100 DAYS

TO LEADERSHIP IMPACT

Casey Reason

100 DAYS
to Leadership
Impact

CASEY REASON

TRIPLE
NICKEL
PRESS

555 North Morton Street
Bloomington, IN 47404

email: info@triplenickelpress.com
www.triplenickelpress.com

Printed in the United States of America

15 14 13 12 11 1 2 3 4 5

FSC
www.fsc.org
MIX
Paper from
responsible sources
FSC® C013483

Library of Congress Control Number: 2011939327

For Artie, Linda, and Lou—
Love has the greatest impact.

Acknowledgments

Ralph Waldo Emerson said that friendship, like the immorality of the soul, is too good to be believed. This book would not have been possible without the encouragement, technical support, and inspiration of numerous friends in my life. Their wisdom informed the ideas and strategies presented throughout this text. Dr. Wesley Avram is a pastor for Pinnacle Presbyterian Church in Scottsdale, Arizona. His ability to thoughtfully inspire me each week while also providing me with thoughtful reflections on his journey in leadership deserves acknowledgment. Ken Blanchard, mentor, friend, and the author of *The One Minute Manager*, continues to inspire me, and it is through his friendship that I made another friend who was particularly impactful in authoring this book. Richard L. Andersen is the president and CEO of Northlands in Edmonton, Alberta. In addition to his deep knowledge of successful leadership practice, Richard was in the early stages of his first 100 days in a new leadership position while I was writing this book. His generosity in sharing his thoughts and perspectives allowed me to continue to flesh out strategies that we both hoped would serve other leaders in the future in their journeys in leadership and service. Finally, the leadership team in my company—made up of Brenna Burghardt, Angie Cucunato, Stephanie Grant, Mara Leahy, Clair Reason, and Karen Tscherne—continues to move and inspire me with their dedication, loyalty, and uncanny ability to work together as one.

Table of Contents

Everyone, Grab a Chisel!

EVERY LEADER WANTS TO be a force for positive change, bringing improvements or even a breakthrough to his or her organization. Leaders want to have a positive leadership impact—and getting off to a good start is key.

This book is for leaders who want to have a powerful leadership impact. Though it's written to give guidance to leaders in their first 100 days of a new position, *100 Days to Leadership Impact* can help leaders at virtually any point in their jobs, preparing them for their first 100 days as well as for day 101 and beyond.

Leaders at every level can make an impact. Gone are the days when a company's only leader was its CEO. Competitive organizations are led by impactful leadership at all levels. The strategies and suggestions in this book are applicable in a variety of settings, regardless of whether you're the CEO. I've taken CEO perspectives and practices into account, but you can use the same material to make an immediate impact from your role as a middle manager or the leader of a much smaller team.

How do leaders make their mark on an organization? Michelangelo believed that his sculpture did not begin with him, but rather that the finished piece already existed within the marble. His job was to *release* the image and make it visible to the outside world. To make that happen, Michelangelo needed an artist's eye, a steady hand, and a series of sharpened chisels and perfectly weighted hammers.

While Michelangelo crafted his timeless masterpieces alone, today's leaders lead, create, and evaluate in collaboration with many other people, both within and outside their own organizations. Thanks to technology, that collaboration occurs at unprecedented speeds and involves many people simultaneously, providing ample opportunity for feedback and input. Leaders are under pressure to quickly decide which contributions they'll incorporate and to what extent—to coordinate the work of numerous contributing artists in real time. They don't just bring their own ideas to the table. Instead, they make an impact by leading everyone to work together to create something new, competitive, and innovative.

Why Another Book on Leadership?

Many leadership books address the strategic steps that new business leaders can take to respond to a myriad of new managerial challenges. This book is less concerned with the immediate, management-oriented crush of activities, focusing instead on how to begin to establish an organizational culture that can lead to real change. *100 Days to Leadership Impact* will help you:

- **Know the leader within.** This book offers opportunities to reflect deeply on your beliefs as a leader and consider ways in which you might grow in the first 100 days in your new role and beyond. To be able to focus on making a powerful leadership impact, leaders must first know themselves and their priorities.

- **Improve performance and results.** There's a difference between performance and results. By improving your performance as a leader, you may not always see the immediate results. You will, however, be laying a foundation for change that will ultimately lead to better results. This book offers Monday-morning-ready, application-oriented strategies designed to have an immediate effect on everyone in your organization.

- **Get off to a great start.** Today's culture has accelerated expectations for immediate feedback and results. Good leaders make speedy impacts. This book will help you prioritize necessary changes and make them quickly.

- **Create a meaningful leadership impact.** We'll examine the concept of creating leadership impacts in contrast to what is presented in traditional leadership models. Establishing your professional practice around creating leadership impacts is far different than simply filling the role of a traditional leader.

- **Build a clear leadership vision.** The concept of leadership vision is often accompanied by rather vague ideas about how a leader should bring clarity of vision to an organization. Even so, a clear vision is an important part of corporate health and progress. Leaders use modern research about individual and collective learning styles to strategically set organizational vision.

- **Survive and thrive during the testing process.** New leaders should expect to be tested early and often. This book explains why this testing process is both necessary and advantageous to both leaders and companies.

- **Stimulate innovation.** The most competitive organizations consistently search for leaders who get individuals and groups thinking out of the box, stimulating the most creative levels of innovation. This book will help you be one of those leaders.

- **Maximize learning and growth opportunities.** By understanding how leaders affect individual and team learning, you can have a much more profound influence on those around you.

- **Build a more connected, trusting culture.** Sustained, meaningful change requires a trusting, connected culture. This book explains some of the challenges leaders face in creating that culture and identifies specific strategies to overcome obstacles.

- **Learn to understand and use key institutional filters and data-gathering techniques.** Veteran leaders rely to a great extent on intuition to observe the information around them. Data is a helpful addition, and this book contains specific data-gathering strategies that leaders can use to observe systems in a way that quickly reveals the best decision-making information.

Why Is Making an Impact Important?

Leaders never take a new job in hopes that their presence won't be noticed. Indeed, leaders anticipate that their arrival will be the catalyst for change and new results.

Leaders in the past tended to see that improvement as a by-product of their direct action. Successful leaders today, however, have learned to lead differently. They've learned that change is driven by organizational culture, and they've developed their ability to act as stealthy architects whose direct and indirect actions ultimately increase system-wide capacity to lead and implement change. It's this new culture that yields improved results throughout the organization, and the impact leaders make is by developing that culture.

Why 100 Days?

Organizations expect that your leadership impact will be felt immediately. Thus the title of this book, *100 Days to Leadership Impact*, suggests that leaders must take their positions with the intention of making a significant impact from the very beginning, quickly establishing the type of leadership culture that can continue to change during the first 100 days and beyond. You've got many more than 100 days ahead of you—but this book focuses on the impact you'll make in your first 100 days in a new leadership role and the momentum and expectations you'll set for day 101 and beyond.

Think of yourself as an artist, ready to unlock the greatness within the stone, as you move into the chapters ahead. Those who see you coming with that hammer and chisel will soon come to expect that they, too, will hammer, chip, and create alongside you.

Let's look at the 100-day timeline. The number of days you spend in each phase may vary by a few days.

The 100-Day Timeline

Phase 1: Days 1–6	Phase 2: Days 7–39	Phase 3: Days 40–69	Phase 4: Days 70–100
Creating a Lasting First Impression	Getting in Motion	Testing and Trusting	Celebrating and Looking Forward

Phase 1: Creating a Lasting First Impression

There is no substitute for the excitement and energy that characterize a leader's first few days on the job, and there's no better time to make a good first impression. Our first exposure to something new establishes the perception from which we will operate from that point on.[1] Get off to a tepid start in your first week, and you'll spend a great deal of time and energy challenging that perception.

Phase 2: Getting in Motion

In the first month or so on the job, a leader learns a great deal about what's going on at an organization. In this second phase, you start taking the actions that will ultimately lead to positive leadership impact.

Phase 3: Testing and Trusting

By six weeks into the job, the leader is fully in motion. You more clearly understand what's going on in the organization, and those around you expect that you are no longer new and confused. They are becoming familiar with your leadership style. You and your colleagues are carefully observing one another and, at times, testing each other's commitments, consistency, and resolve.

Phase 4: Celebrating and Looking Forward

By the end of the first 70 days or so, a new organizational culture has been established. The new leadership impacts will become increasingly obvious with each passing day. For an ineffective leader, this is the point when the wheels begin to fall off the wagon; the changes are short-lived. An effective leader, however, now sees new habits developing and better patterns emerging consistently. These last 30 days are a time for key observations of progress, notation of needed adjustments, and preparation for the culmination of the first 100 days.

Organization of the Book

This book can be utilized in two ways. You certainly can jump from chapter to chapter and pick up some valuable information about leadership. However, if you read the book chapter by chapter, you will see that it defines a purposeful 100-day trajectory to leadership impact.

Each chapter outlines specific steps you can take to prepare you for the next phases of development.

In chapters 1 and 2, I will more specifically define what I mean by *leadership impact*. I will show you how to explore your own leadership priorities and create what this book refers to as your *leadership dashboard*. By the end of chapters 1 and 2, you will have done your homework and will be ready for your arrival. Chapter 3 then discusses the all-important first impression and provides strategies you can implement in phase 1 to make your first impression positive, powerful, and lasting.

In chapters 4 and 5, I will address the steps you can take to move into phase 2 of your first 100 days. You will learn how to collect and analyze information on the current organizational culture and the individual and collective mental models that drive employee perceptions. Then you can begin to thoughtfully consider the steps you must take immediately to reshape the status quo where needed.

Chapters 6, 7, and 8 explore the steps you can take to excel in the testing and trusting phase, phase 3. Specifically, we will look at the steps contemporary leaders take to clarify their vision and to recognize when, in fact, the new leadership impact is being tested or challenged.

Finally, in chapters 9 and 10, we will examine some of the steps you can take to identify the fruits of your labors in phase 4 and build real learning power by maximizing growth opportunities. Having laid the foundation for your leadership impact, your next step is to sustain it.

Seize the Day

This book is thoughtfully designed for the busy leadership practitioner. It's full of high-impact, easily applied leadership strategies that you can quickly absorb and apply right away. After reading this book, you will know how to make a significant leadership impact that results in a much more connected culture, fueled by increased team capacity to innovate and real learning power. Get ready to lead like never before. It's time to seize day 1 of your 100 days!

Chapter 1

Creating a
Leadership Impact

No LEADER EVER DREAMS of making things worse. Leaders take on new positions with optimism and a desire to make things better. In fact, the best leaders begin their work with clear ideas about the leadership impact they'd like to make and the metrics they'll use to measure changes that show their impact.

Take a moment to think about your own vision and potential metrics. Will you measure your positive leadership impact in profits? Customer satisfaction? Employee satisfaction?

This chapter will help you define your leadership impact and explain the steps you can take to influence the organizational culture in a positive way—starting immediately. The 100-day timeline shows the four phases of the journey toward making that all-important impact. Throughout *100 Days to Leadership Impact* we will continue to reference this timeline to help you conceptualize each phase of your development moving forward.

The 100-Day Timeline

Phase 1: Days 1–6	Phase 2: Days 7–39	Phase 3: Days 40–69	Phase 4: Days 70–100
Creating a Lasting First Impression	Getting in Motion	Testing and Trusting	Celebrating and Looking Forward

Picture This

I often ask workshop participants to draw a picture of what they see when they visualize a powerful leadership impact. Pictures are powerful tools, showing what's really in our heads and illustrating how we see the world.

As I've done this exercise with hundreds of audiences around the world, some interesting similarities have emerged. In many cases, workshop participants draw images of people. Sometimes they draw a group, arm in arm in some sort of synergistic dance, all celebrating the leadership impact, and sometimes they single out one figure as a leader. More than half the time the leader portrayed in these illustrations is male. He is often shown hovering above others, gazing at them in paternal approval. Even when participants use abstract images to illustrate leadership impacts, in fact, they tend to create hierarchical pictures that show the relationships between individuals at graduated responsibility levels.

As we discuss the pictures, participants often conclude that they think of leadership impacts in relation to the direct actions a leader in a specific position might take. They imagine that leadership is a direct result of what the leader does in that position.

A leadership impact can be much more subtle and less tangible, however. Although most organizations do experience times when traditional leaders must stand up and assert themselves in ways we typically associate with leadership behavior, the most successful organizations have come to recognize that the deepest change often comes as a result of an emerging leadership culture, not a single person. This culture seems to vibrate throughout the organization, energizing *everyone* to do and become more. The best leaders reshape how others view their challenges, approach their work, and treat each other by focusing on building this leadership culture. This more powerful approach to leadership impact creates an invisible force that can change the organization in focused, dramatic ways—and manifests itself even when the leader isn't there in person.

Understanding Strong Leadership

The concept of leadership impact has developed around a handful of seminal leadership theories and emerging schools of thought regarding leading, learning, collaboration, and change. It's important to understand its foundational concepts.

The Best Leadership Is Transformational

Transformational leaders inspire those around them to see their challenges with new eyes and to imagine that their efforts will truly transform a situation. Transformational leaders stir a deeper sense of belief and move others to see their inspiration and opportunity. A transformational leader tries to inspire deep, substantive changes that produce dramatically improved outcomes.

Leaders Serve Others

As defined by scholars Robert Greenleaf[1] and Ken Blanchard,[2] *servant leaders* try to create intense leadership impacts by focusing on other people. In their vision, the most profound leadership impacts emerge when a leader serves others, encouraging and supporting them to become their best. In doing so, they create a more connected culture—one that is likely to produce positive outcomes. Despite the term *servant*, servant leaders are very much in charge and must be able to manage and redirect those around them.

Leadership Is Focused on Learning

The past twenty-five years have seen significant focus on organizational learning. The most competitive companies are those that can learn something new, grow, and adapt in response to change. Therefore, one of the most important leadership measures is the degree to which a leader inspires individual and team learning.

Leadership Is a Force, Not a Position

Well-led organizations don't depend on a domineering taskmaster who bullies the best out of everyone involved. The best organizations involve adults working together toward new goals and outcomes, with the leader often working collaboratively alongside everybody else.

The leadership energy you bring to your organization is an important tool—one that can help you make deep changes and improve outcomes.

Making Your Own Leadership Impact

Because it is my intent in this book to teach you to make a more significant leadership impact in your first 100 days, I want to remind you that this impact must be your own. While others may have some ideas about what they hope a leader in your position will bring, your capacity to exercise some level of influence over the environment is driven to a great extent by your personality, values, priorities, and the mental models that shape your perspective.

While any leader reading this book would agree that creating a leadership impact is certainly desirable, we sometimes have a difficult time getting clear about what establishing a leadership impact actually means. For the purposes of this book, we will define leadership impact as manifesting in two ways: building a connected culture and developing real learning power within the organization.

Build a Connected Culture

As discussed earlier, transformational and servant leaders create safe, focused, collaborative working environments. That takes sustained effort—effort that never really ends. The degree to which you begin creating that environment in your first 100 days largely determines your ultimate leadership impact.

It's difficult to measure a culture's connected qualities. Positive, productive organizations seem to have an emotional hum, a sense that employees find comfort and connection with one another. You can take steps to deliberately create this atmosphere.

- **Make collaboration non-negotiable.** Most organizations today must work fast; they move forward thanks to highly collaborative networks of teams constantly working together. Leaders must consistently reinforce the notion that collaboration is a non-negotiable, everlasting working condition that drives systemic success.

  Despite all that's been written about the power of collaboration, some organizations are still filled with solo acts. Such organizations may push back when employees are suddenly expected to work in teams, especially during your first 100 days. In order for collaboration to be meaningful, we must keep in mind that some work is best done alone, and there is no substitute for deep individual reflection. Consistent, open collaboration, however, brings a level of honesty, energy, and balance to just about every organization, and transformational leadership is dependent on opportunities to interact.

Early forays into collaboration can actually create discord in previously peaceful organizations. Leaders may need to be patient, maintaining a work-appropriate collaborative expectation. You'll ultimately see a more connected culture in which problems are resolved, not ignored.

- **Confront the bully.** Some organizations have resident bullies who find power through intimidation. Left unchecked, bullying behavior can create a toxic and fearful environment where collaboration and creativity cannot emerge. You must be brave enough to confront bullies and insist that a connected culture cannot sustain their behavior.

- **Break the ice.** It can take a bit of courage to talk to someone you don't know. In getting to know a stranger, you must extend yourself. New leaders must break the icy tension of uncertainty that comes with facing someone or something new. Visualize yourself breaking ice everywhere you go in your first 100 days.

- **Make connection a sacred value.** What we do is more important than what we say, but it's still necessary to verbally reiterate the importance of building a supportive, connected culture. Make sure your team knows that you value connecting and collaborating, and that you see both as integral to the impact you hope to make.

- **Laugh and listen.** Leaders who laugh send a powerful message. Laugh at yourself, and you show others that you're human. They may begin to believe that they can be human around you, too. Listening is one of the most powerful ways to build a connection with someone. Don't multitask while someone else is speaking. Show others that you are emotionally invested in what they say. Remember important conversational details.

- **Let others lead.** Being out of control at work is a bad feeling, like skidding your car on the ice. Uncompromising, domineering leaders create the fear that they may force us into uncomfortable, difficult, or even painful situations without considering our thoughts, needs, and feelings. We know our survival is not on the line, but our brains have a difficult time differentiating between actual fear and the psychological fear associated with things that make us nervous and afraid.[3] When it's appropriate, let others lead. They'll relax when they see that they have some control and aren't operating at the boss's moment-by-moment pleasure.

- **Establish values and beliefs.** Every action you take demonstrates your values and beliefs, revealing where you stand as a leader. Arrive at your leadership challenge knowing your own values and beliefs, and do your best to understand how your actions reinforce those positions. Remember, too, that every organization has institutionalized values and beliefs. Identify those organizational values and beliefs. Are they the values and beliefs that will take the company to the next performance level?

- **Establish accountability at all levels.** Accountability is essential. It can be as simple as agreed-upon deadlines with opportunities to give and receive feedback along the way. More complex qualitative feedback opportunities can also help keep things on track. Leaders who value open and authentic communication must have accountability measures that allow anyone to call out anyone else when work systems fail or when anyone at any level fails to meet expectations. Values and beliefs are powerful, but accountability makes the pursuit of loftier aspirations possible.

Develop Learning Power

As with building a connected culture, developing learning power within an organization is a never-ending process. Consider this process as a tool for creating leadership impact. A variety of strategies can help.

- **Talk openly about the merits of individual and team learning.** The healthiest organizations consistently and accurately assess their own learning power. They talk openly about the things they know, the things they haven't yet learned, and how their learning is progressing.

- **Develop learning spaces and sacred learning time.** People need time and space to learn. Some environments support this better than others. Dark, noisy, distracting places, especially with uncomfortable temperature and climate swings, aren't good places to learn. Bright, quiet, comfortable spaces, on the other hand, promote learning. Furthermore, any good leader understands that actually scheduling an action makes it real. Many leaders claim that reflection is important, but far too few actually make time for it. Impactful leaders interested in developing real learning power schedule and protect time for deep thinking.

- **Apply learning as often as possible.** It's frustrating to learn something and never use it again. Wise leaders seek out ways to apply new lessons during their first 100 days. Employees who understand that the organization expects them to learn and use material in real situations take the job of learning much more seriously, evolving in a more direct, focused fashion.

- **Take training seriously.** Make sure participants get training details before they attend. Identify learning objectives, and give participants ways to offer feedback on the training itself. Better yet, when possible, allow participants to choose training topics and modalities. This tends to increase engagement in the learning process.

- **Reward learning *and* outcomes.** The bottom line will always be important, but learning new things that aren't immediately applicable is important, too. Call out learning opportunities, and talk about the growth under way. Ask colleagues, "What are you learning? How will the new learning be applied? What can we expect?" Rewarding individual and team learners helps make learning a more integral part of the organization.

- **Monitor emotions on an ongoing basis.** Emotion is the genesis of all individual and collective learning.[4] To truly manage an organization's learning power, you must consistently monitor the group's emotional tenor. We'll talk later about emotions that stimulate and those that derail the learning process. Leaders who are consistently aware of emotions, however, have mastered a key first step.

At your interviews with staff and during your first few days of work, your intention to build a culture of learning and collaboration should be a point of conversation. In phase 2, as you begin to take direct action, you must once again grab every opportunity to promote your intended leadership impact. This will be especially true during phase 3, when you will no doubt be tested and challenged. Organization members will want to see whether you truly are dedicated to your leadership vision, or if are you simply giving lip service until the pressure is on. Phase 4 brings rewards if you've convinced your teammates that you are committed to a leadership impact that takes you through and beyond the first 100 days.

Key Terms

Leadership impact

Transformational leadership

Servant leadership

Connected culture

Learning power

Questions for Reflection

1. What kind of leadership impact did my predecessor make?

2. How can I develop a connected culture?

3. How can I stimulate deep levels of learning?

4. What can I do to demonstrate my dedication to transformational expectations as I lead this organization?

5. How can we demonstrate a more service-oriented philosophy?

Chapter 2

Designing Your Leadership Dashboard

WHERE DO YOU LOOK when you're driving?

The best drivers consistently and simultaneously monitor several vision points. They've learned to systematically shift their glance from the road ahead to the rearview mirror, side mirror, speedometer, and then other essential gauges. They may monitor the road ahead and the speedometer with greater intensity and frequency than other gauges on the dashboard; after all, not every gauge is equally important at every moment of the journey. That said, they are sure to check every gauge at least occasionally.

Drivers who are less effective behind the wheel have not developed the habit of monitoring the most important gauges. They are distracted—by satellite radio, cell phones, text messages, accidents on the other side of the highway, or outdated GPS directions. They've taken their attention away from the most important task: driving.

Good leaders are a lot like good drivers: they remain alert, observe the road ahead, and have learned to consistently and systematically monitor the most essential measures. But your new job doesn't come factory-equipped with a dashboard of the most important measures of your progress. Instead, you have to develop your own leadership dashboard of the "gauges" you believe are most essential to your organization and your leadership goals. You also have to establish which of them you will monitor with greater frequency as you continue to scan the road ahead.

All leaders have dashboards. Inexperienced leaders might let others design their dashboards, telling them where to put their time and attention. Experienced leaders, on the other hand, develop their own leadership dashboards—ones that sustain them in a variety of leadership settings. If you don't build your own leadership dashboard, other people will be glad to build it for you. You may not like the results.

This chapter is designed to fortify your preparation to lead in the first 100 days. By understanding your capacity to establish a leadership impact, and by giving some thought to the dashboard elements that you will consistently monitor as a leader, you will ready yourself for those all-important first days on the job. As you design your leadership dashboard, give yourself some flexibility; know that your dashboard elements may have to change over time as new priorities and focal points emerge.

The 100-Day Timeline

Phase 1: Days 1–6	Phase 2: Days 7–39	Phase 3: Days 40–69	Phase 4: Days 70–100
Creating a Lasting First Impression	Getting in Motion	Testing and Trusting	Celebrating and Looking Forward

Who's the Boss?

Hank had a difficult first 100 days. He arrived as a young middle-level manager in one of the largest hospitals in the city of Chicago, hoping to bring substantive change to what appeared to be an under-performing work team.

Hank listened attentively as other leaders and team veterans suggested where his priorities and focus should lie. They thought he should take every opportunity to communicate with his constituents, so Hank set up an aggressive, time-consuming meeting schedule. He heard that his predecessor had not communicated well, and he was determined to operate differently.

In his first month on the job, during phase 2 of his first 100 days, Hank realized that he was overcommitted, but he had promised to meet with constituents and listen well. Backing out of meetings would send the message that he was not really so committed to communication.

The crush of work moved in, and Hank's meeting commitments continued to clog his calendar. Each week was filled with one meeting after another, and Hank found himself tired and confused about where he should put his energy each day. His time was no longer his own, and so many problems were waiting.

Hank let other people, both in person and via email, determine his priorities. That didn't give him a lot of time or energy to do what *he* thought was important. By determining your leadership priorities ahead of time, you take control.

What's on Your Dashboard?

Leadership dashboards are personal and unique. Your dashboard elements are based in part on who you are as a person, then on your priorities as a leader. With experience you'll likely develop a general dashboard that serves you well in many situations, but you'll also add elements that are unique to each new leadership situation. Some priorities will evolve as you spend time on the job. You may not know about the need for new sales targets when you arrive, for example. Other dashboard items, such as promoting collaboration and learning, apply in virtually every leadership situation.

Enter phase 1 with a working sense of your leadership priorities and metrics. Doing so keeps your eye on your goals. It also gives you great talking points as you meet your new colleagues. Meet with a new manager to talk about building community. Chat with the sales team about how they collaborate. Your team will hear your priorities. As you move through your first 100 days, a continued focus on priorities helps you build credibility. Colleagues begin to trust that your spoken priorities are real points of focus—not just hot air.

What are your leadership priorities? How do your general leadership focal points differ from your priorities for this particular situation? Your list might include:

- Promoting learning, collaboration, and service
- Expanding profit margins, containing costs, and improving daily operations
- Promoting creativity and innovation
- Building community with values and beliefs
- Identifying and pursuing new markets
- Meeting annual sales goals
- Staying accountable to projected goals
- Consistently communicating progress
- Finding creativity in everyone

Some of the items on this list might be part of your personal goals, or at least could serve as priorities in virtually any leadership situation—even one that changes quickly. Promoting collaboration and service, building community, supporting creativity and innovation, and consistently communicating mission and goals are relatively universal concepts, for instance, though they can get left behind if a leader does not deliberately promote them. Other potential dashboard items may be more particular to a single leadership situation.

Limit your dashboard to seven or eight items. Your list will evolve with your leadership style; job-specific items will come and go. Overall, however, your dashboard elements will probably stay with you for years to come, helping define you as a leader. Each priority is either based on the leader's values and beliefs—which demonstrate your leadership style—or a key part of establishing the accountability and persistence any effective organization needs. For example, the bulleted list given earlier focuses on building a connected culture and developing learning power. Promoting learning, collaboration, and service, building community based on values and beliefs, and consistently communicating progress are all steps leaders can take to promote a connected culture. Leaders who champion creativity and innovation promote learning power.

Put Your Dashboard Where You Can See It

It's so easy to get wrapped up in the daily crush of emails, projects, travel, and other priorities. Many leaders look up one day and realize that's it's been quite some time since they worried about promoting a creative and innovative environment or went out of their way to evaluate the degree to which a team is learning and collaborating. Make these moments of neglect less frequent by putting your leadership dashboard where you can literally see it.

I carry a leadership dashboard that uses symbols to represent each priority.

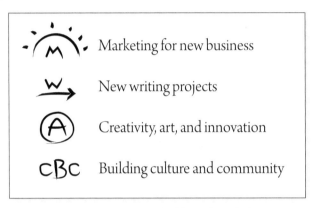

Casey's leadership dashboard symbols.

Write down your dashboard elements, and post them somewhere you can see them: on your office wall or in your calendar, perhaps. Find a way to put your dashboard in front of your eyes every day so it can remind you of all the priorities that require your attention.

Where Are You Going?

On a cross-country road trip, you know you're getting close to your destination when you see the city limits sign. Once you know your priorities, how can you tell whether your organization is realizing them? Maybe you intend to build community. What will you observe to determine if your organization is making progress in building community?

Some dashboard priorities lend themselves to formal metrics. You'll know that your organization is successfully identifying and pursuing new markets, for instance, when you can point to a given number of newly identified markets and enumerate the steps your organization has taken to pursue them.

Other dashboard priorities aren't so easy to measure. Think about ways you might know that the company is making progress in those areas. You might make creative problem solving a priority, for instance. Maybe you'll know that you're making progress when you begin to hear new, innovative strategies as you move from one conversation to another. Even qualitative or anecdotal feedback in a priority area helps leaders focus on the areas that matter most.

Reflecting on Your Dashboard Elements

Don't just identify your dashboard elements and keep them under your nose. Challenge yourself to *make progress* in each identified area. Wouldn't it be exciting if you made even a little progress in each area every month? Every quarter? Every year? There will always be times when you fall short. Balance those moments by looking at your dashboard priorities and realizing that you did actually build community and promote learning and collaboration—maybe by using an opportunity you never could have anticipated. Make a date with yourself to sit down and think about what you are doing. It's time well spent, especially in your first 100 days.

Having your dashboard elements nearby can be a constant source of motivation. I find myself renewed as I think about my dashboard elements, and I regularly stop to reflect on the progress I've made. When I identify growth, I invariably get momentum and find myself more determined than ever to look for new leadership and growth opportunities.

As you reflect on each dashboard element, consider:

- Why is this element important?
- What is my destination?
- How am I progressing?
- Am I out of balance? Are certain areas growing well while others lag?

- What can I do this year, quarter, week, or day to make progress in this area?
- What am I proud of? What should my team be proud of?
- How do my dashboard elements help create a connected culture?
- How do my dashboard elements improve learning power?

Your own leadership experience will inform your dashboard, as can conversations with mentors, peers, and other trusted advisors.

Key Terms

| Leadership dashboard
| Dashboard elements

Questions for Reflection

1. What are my leadership dashboard focal points?

2. What specific steps am I taking to keep my dashboard elements close to me?

3. Are others aware of my dashboard elements? Do they know why these elements are important to me?

Chapter 3

Creating a Lasting First Impression

BEGINNING A NEW JOB is an intense experience. It's no wonder that most people focus on their own experience during their first days. Just remember that your colleagues will focus on their own experiences, too—their experiences and first impressions of you.

Most people try hard to make a good impression. And yet it's surprisingly easy to fail, often for reasons the new leader doesn't understand. The first few hours and days of your new job are key to making a positive impression that will make other people eager to follow your lead. It's certainly possible to overcome a bad start, but beginning well gives you the opportunity to generate momentum in a much shorter period of time.

The 100-Day Timeline

Phase 1: Days 1–6	Phase 2: Days 7–39	Phase 3: Days 40–69	Phase 4: Days 70–100
Creating a Lasting First Impression	Getting in Motion	Testing and Trusting	Celebrating and Looking Forward

You have worked hard to prepare for this moment. As you begin phase 1 of your journey with new colleagues, the steps you take and the choices you make in your first few days on the job will begin to immediately demonstrate the leadership impact you are likely to make moving forward. This is the start of an important four-stage process, and getting off to a strong start will make a big difference!

An Unintended Message

As Carrie prepared for her new position as division leader of Star Industries' largest factory, she was filled with excitement and anticipation. Star Industries designed and produced some key components to modern antilock breaking systems. It had been a preferred supplier to a prominent U.S. car manufacturer for almost 30 years. Carrie's position was unique in that she had a chance to work with white-collar management as well as to connect with frontline production. As a younger member of management, she saw this as a great opportunity to learn more about the production side of the business while simultaneously building up her background and skills as a leader.

Carrie wanted to present herself as the consummate professional to her new colleagues. When she arrived at the factory, her hair was styled appropriately and her nails manicured. She wore an expensive business suit, a new watch, and a tasteful pair of well-made shoes. Under her arm she toted the new mobile tablet. Her dexterity with this pricey piece of technology was impressive to anyone who watched her work. Carrie hoped that her technological fluency, professional presentation, and quick wit would serve to reinforce the message that, despite her age and limited experience, she was the right person for the job.

Carrie knew her leadership challenge was going to be difficult. The company was in dire financial straits, and there had been staffing and salary cutbacks just before her arrival. This was a major advancement in Carrie's career, and she knew that success at this level could mean great things for her in the company in the years to come. She saw the investment in her tablet and updated business attire as a statement to all observers that she deserved a seat at the table. Her brand-new BMW 3 Series, which she drove to work, likewise made a statement to her colleagues that she had arrived and was a reminder to her each day of how hard she had worked to get to this point so early in her career.

Through her first days and weeks, Carrie greeted colleagues with a bright smile and a firm handshake. Her expensive timepiece glistened under the lights of the factory floor. In each meeting she popped open her electronic tablet to jot notes. She felt certain that her professionalism was making a good impression on her new colleagues.

But to Carrie's surprise, she began to feel coolness from some of her colleagues. With each passing day, the reception appeared less friendly.

One of the challenges leaders face when taking on a new position is others' suspicion that the new leader isn't fully invested in the organization's coming challenges, but rather is using the leadership position as a self-serving stepping stone toward some loftier perch in the company or beyond. The cold reception that Carrie received no doubt resulted from her lack of awareness of the company culture she had inherited. For despite the fact that for her life was good and this promotion meant new levels of fiscal autonomy for her, most of her colleagues were not enjoying similar prosperity. Her expensive celebratory shopping spree might have made her feel like a leader, but it made those around her see her as an outsider who didn't understand their challenges. As a result, Carrie failed to make that all-important good first impression.

Projecting Your Leadership Image

The first impressions you make teach those around you who you are and how you intend to lead. Think of your first impressions from a marketing perspective: know what you intend to market, how you should present it, and why that choice is particularly important or effective in this environment. How will you make your arrival have impact?

Consider Your Company's Current Situation

Based on what you know about your job, you may believe that you were brought into this leadership situation to bring calm to an already chaotic environment. How can you present yourself as a calm person who is able to lead your organization into less troubled times? Maybe skipping that second cup of coffee keeps you from sounding wired and rushed, or perhaps you find ways to simplify routines and provide calm clarification of expectations and opportunities. On the other hand, if innovation and breakthough are the goals, perhaps you make sure that you are seen enthusiastically learning and applying a new piece of technology that will help you learn and do more.

Commit to Collection

In your first 100 days, what you collect is just as important as what you project. Look around. Your fresh perspective will only last a little while, so observe and reflect on everything you can. This is your opportunity to gather information with perhaps the most authentic set of outside eyes you will ever have. Take notes on what you observe, either on paper or using a digital recorder.

Go Mobile

Well-intended administrative assistants may set up meetings for constituents to greet you in your new office. Extemporaneous drop-ins are fine, but don't let meetings trap you in your office. You need to learn about your organization's culture firsthand.

Get out of your office. Visit others at their sites. Make yourself visible. By doing so, you'll meet people in the spaces where they feel most comfortable, project your intended leadership image to a larger number of people, and collect more information from those you encounter along the way—and you'll probably learn much more from those informal encounters than you would in formal meetings. Going mobile also sends the message that you are willing to meet people halfway (or all the way!) if necessary.

Note Names and Details

This simple suggestion isn't new, but it's still worth the effort. Remembering people's names and details about their lives will move you closer to each of your constituents and help you gain their trust—an essential part of convincing them to extend themselves on your behalf. It's hard to trust someone who doesn't know your name, but much easier if the leader remembers not just your name, but also the name of your spouse, child, or beloved pet. Make the connection genuine, not manipulative. Share your own appropriate personal details. When you connect on a human level, it's much easier to work toward shared professional goals.

Make Your Dashboard Components Your Talking Points

By this point you will have developed your leadership dashboard. Some dashboard elements will change during your first 100 days, but many others will remain constant. Be ready to talk about these dashboard elements early and often. Develop talking points about what they mean to you.

Unchanging priorities, such as developing a collaborative environment or increasing the system's capacity to learn new things, become a benchmark for your leadership identity. When they hear your message early and often, colleagues will understand that you are focused, sincere, and determined. (Dashboard talking points can also offer a way to keep a lagging conversation going.)

Learn About the Organization's History

As you develop a clear leadership vision for your organization, you'll need to understand the system's history. Explore whatever information you can find. As you visit colleagues during your first few days of work, ask questions about the organization's recent and more distant past. Look for trends, listen carefully, and write down your observations as you begin to learn how history has played into the current working situation. You will work with others who are still responding to the organization's history. The more you understand that history, the better you will be able to comprehend the present and plan for the future.

Look for Current Context

History gives you perspective on how things came to be. An organization's current reality, however, is even more important than its history. Carrie's coworkers didn't react to the record-breaking profits the company made ten years ago; they responded to the recent cutbacks. Carrie should have understood that, despite once having been very profitable, her company was in financial trouble. That reality dictated her wisest path forward. A company's current context and its immediate challenges are a more accurate indicator of its future than are the glory—or gory—days of the past.

As you arrive, think about capturing an initial snapshot that shows you the organization's current context. We'll talk more about how to do this later.

Try to See Yourself in the Group

To avoid making the mistake that Carrie made as illustrated earlier in the chapter, try to imagine how others are seeing you interact in the organization. Think about the impression you may be making—your projected leadership image—and reflect on your interaction patterns and the things you are doing to represent who you are and what your priorities are.

As you become experienced, it is also helpful to be thoughtful about the kind of culture you are intuitively sensing and the steps you can take as a leader to immediately respond. For example, if you sense upon your arrival that the organization is rather stiff and unfriendly, you may find yourself attempting to introduce a greater degree of warmth and connection through your interactions. You will likely be more successful at improving this weak spot in the organization if you act on your perception gradually at first and allow it to build momentum over time. Likewise, if you sense that the system is rather disorganized and chaotic, you may decide to proactively communicate a sense of calmness and bring structured simplicity to your interactions.

Knowing what is needed isn't always easy, and your ideas may change over time. But keep in mind that if you can sense a particular area of need or systemic weakness, others likely feel it as well. If an environment has been consistently stressful and chaotic, your ability to express rational, focused simplicity will be intuitively appreciated—and your leadership impact will begin to shape new organizational patterns.

Being a Teacher and a Network Specialist

As you think about nurturing a collaborative, connected culture with significant levels of learning power, imagine yourself arriving on the scene as a teacher and network specialist.

Think of the most creative, meaningful instructor you ever had. That teacher probably created an environment where learning happened organically and students pursued it with passion and curiosity. How would your favorite teacher get everyone thinking? How would that teacher stimulate class members to do and become more? That's the teacher you want to be.

A network specialist ensures that systems are up and running each day, with devices ready to connect at a moment's notice. Leaders are network specialists, ensuring high levels of connectivity and bandwidth at all levels.

Key Terms

> Arrival impact
>
> Mobility and visibility
>
> Projected leadership image
>
> History
>
> Snapshot
>
> Prevailing individual and collective mental models

Questions for Reflection

1. What do I hope my constituents will say about me after our first meeting?

2. How must I prepare for my arrival in order to project the appropriate message about my leadership mission and goals?

3. What thoughts, ideas, data, and/or talking points must I have in mind to shape initial conversations and create the impact I imagine?

Chapter 4

Taking a Company Snapshot

As a leader, you know it's a mistake to confuse action with progress. Your new team will be eager to make a good impression on you. When we're unsure about what the leader wants and how a new leadership vision will affect us and our company, most people default to hard work and furious action as a way of demonstrating their value.

Hardworking constituents, of course, are a great resource, and it's terrific that they want to make a good impression on you. It's more important, however, that you make sure that your team is working hard *on the right priorities.* And adjusting to new priorities can be hard on a workforce.

You are now in phase 2 of your first 100 days, and your leadership impact is getting in motion! While the process of taking a company snapshot described in this chapter may seem like a formative step in which the leader is primarily observing and questioning, keep in mind that you continue to deepen your leadership impact with the passing of each day. First, the process of getting to know your team by following these steps will help them to begin to better understand you and, perhaps, to connect with you on a more human level. Second, by asking deep, substantive questions about key elements of their jobs, you will reinforce the notion that creating a leadership *force* is everyone's responsibility. As people reflect thoughtfully on your questions, they will realize that you are deeply interested in their knowledge of their work, their investment in the organizational culture and climate, their learning power, and the new learning objectives that lie ahead for everyone.

The 100-Day Timeline

Phase 1: Days 1–6 Creating a Lasting First Impression	Phase 2: Days 7–39 Getting in Motion	Phase 3: Days 40–69 Testing and Trusting	Phase 4: Days 70–100 Celebrating and Looking Forward

A Question of Priorities

Charles is the head of the security guards at the Jackson State Penitentiary. On top of what is already a very stressful job, Charles has become increasingly frustrated lately with Victor, the new warden. Ever since his arrival a month and a half ago, Victor has been constantly peppering Charles with questions. What makes these inquiries frustrating is that Victor always seems to be asking Charles to clarify his priorities and leadership objectives.

Based on his work with the previous warden and his evaluations up to this point, Charles sees himself as an extremely hardworking, focused, and accomplished prison official. He wonders why Victor is being so intrusive. "Does he think I'm lazy?" Charles thought. "Does he think I don't know what goes on around here? Does he think I don't know what is important?" Finally Charles decided to confront Victor about these constant inquires at their next weekly meeting.

When the meeting began, Charles started talking fast, giving a lengthy and rather breathless summary of his projects and priorities. He listed the recent meetings he'd held and all the actions he had taken to exert influence on his situation.

Victor couldn't help but notice that as Charles discussed his priorities, his tone was a bit anxious, perhaps defensive. At a breaking point in the conversation, Victor said, "From looking at your calendar and watching you work, I can see that you clearly do not lack work ethic in any way. That's a really great quality, one to be admired."

Puzzled, Charles asked, "Then why are you questioning everything that I do? Why are you always asking me what my priorities are? I've worked here a long time, and I know what I'm doing!"

Victor paused for a moment before responding, in case Charles had any more thoughts to add. Finally he replied, "Charles, I think you know that simply working hard isn't enough. We have to make sure that all of us, including me, are working hard on the *right* things. We all have real limits in the time we have to give and the energies we can bring each day to the job. Aligning our energies and efforts in the most effective way is our best tool. Our job now is to work together to make sure that everyone in the organization knows his or her role and is pulling together in a way that gives us the best chance to be successful. Our challenges keep changing, and if we don't consistently communicate, we might be wasting our time and talents. The job of reflecting on our priorities never ends. Doesn't that make sense?"

Sometimes a new leader asks tough questions about priorities and finds that very little needs to change. In other situations, a lot may need to change. When these kinds of discussions haven't been held in a while, workers can easily misinterpret emerging signals or changes in the system and establish priorities that aren't consistent with the development of a better way forward. For that reason, leaders must consistently explore what workers are currently doing, how they're doing it, and how the organization responds in times of change.

Exploring the Snapshot Process

Beginning here and continuing in chapters 5 and 6, and then again in chapters 8 and 10, I will spend some time articulating a specific leadership protocol for the first 100 days that I call the *snapshot process*. The snapshot process allows leaders to systematically (1) gather essential information about the individual work of team members and (2) establish some quick systemic levels of understanding regarding how the team works together. This powerful process allows leaders to also increase their leadership impact by collaborating individually and collectively with the team to construct a more connected community and, ultimately, identify opportunities to develop real learning power.

This snapshot process occurs in five steps taken over the 100-day timeline, as shown in the graphic.

The 100-Day Timeline

Step 1	Step 2	Step 3	Step 4	Step 5
Phase 1: Days 1–6 Creating a Lasting First Impression	Phase 2: Days 7–39 Getting in Motion	Phase 3: Days 40–69 Testing and Trusting	Phase 4: Days 70–100 Celebrating and Looking Forward	

There are five steps to the process; at each step, you'll have meetings with staff that form a snapshot of the company.

1. **Introductory interviews.** Depending on the size of the institution, the leader should attempt to meet individually with all key team members to gather information about their work and their perceptions about the company.

2. **Sharing findings and goal setting.** After gathering copious amounts of information in step 1, the leader will share his or her findings with the larger group and immediately start working with that team to set a goal or goals. Steps 1 and 2 are completed quickly—by end of the leader's first 10 days.

3. **First progress check.** In phase 3, in order to keep momentum going, the leader will check back in with the team and get input on the status of key issues and progress toward the goals defined in step 2.

4. **Second progress check.** Later, the leader will conduct yet another check using the same protocol from step 3, both to measure progress again and to demonstrate commitment to the goals and key emerging issues.

5. **100-day culmination.** Step 5 will take place at or about day 100 and will give the team an opportunity to reflect on and discuss

the progress they have made on the important goals established at the step 2 meeting.

Let's begin by exploring strategies to prepare for the first snapshot.

Step 1: Introductory Interviews

Many of us have been given job descriptions that were already outdated on the day we were hired. Or perhaps the job changed in a matter of weeks or months, taking our priorities in unexpected directions. By the end of phase 1 of your first 100 days, you must start learning what your workers are already doing, then decide how well their current priorities align with the organization's most urgent priorities. To do this, you'll have brief, snapshot conversations with key team members.

Snapshot interviews give a leader an in-the-moment glance at what is happening in an organization. By using them, you'll try to quickly capture as much information as you can about what key individuals do in your company. Your questions will help you learn about your workers, and they'll also help your workers learn about you—for example, that you're interested in listening!—and your leadership style.

If you're leading a group of ten people, you may be able to have snapshot interviews with each of them. But if you're a CEO with hundreds of people reporting to you either directly or indirectly, you won't have time to interview every employee. For large groups, begin by identifying and interviewing your key constituents. Err on the side of interviewing too many people. If the organization is very large, with many key constituents, you may choose to have other leaders conduct some of the snapshot interviews.

Plan Timing With Care

Snapshot interviews should begin just after the first three to five days of introductions. Most of the questions are best answered on the spot, to ensure that interviewees don't have too much time to screen their responses. The final step of the interview process that we'll describe may require some advance preparation and could be conducted individually or in groups, depending on your organization and its work structure.

You might be tempted to give interviewees more time to prepare. Don't, or you'll hear from some type-A personalities who will spend an inordinate amount of time preparing for their interviews. Get off to a fast start. The earlier you get started, the more information you'll have.

Plan to spend 45–90 minutes on each interview; you'll need to spend more time interviewing the employees who hold positions with more complex duties.

Ask Key Questions

Ask the following questions.

1. **Based on your job description, what's your job?** This question is intended to reveal the job the individual was given at hiring, but some interviewees may have gotten very little explanation and found themselves working on whatever needed doing. The response will also give you some insight regarding the degree to which the company has followed job descriptions in recent years.

2. **What are your real job responsibilities?** Pay attention both to what the interviewee does and to how much the answer differs from the person's official job description.

3. **For optimal effectiveness, what should be your job responsibilities be?** The response will show how strategically and comprehensively the interviewee understands the job.

   Listen with extraordinary care. Many people will give answers that tell you much more than the question initially requested. For example, an individual who explains how much more he could do if everyone else just did their jobs shows you how teammates at your organization communicate and collaborate. Some interviewees might blame your predecessor or some aspect of the organization that keeps them where they are—an answer that shows that blame is part of the corporate culture, a potential challenge to your leadership impact.

   In the best case, answers to this question will reveal thoughtful consideration about how jobs might change. You may hear myriad creative solutions—a creative and comprehensive laundry list of new steps workers could take, right now, that could make a positive difference. A formal interview process helps you notice and potentially implement these ideas.

4. **What's working?** Ask the question broadly, and let the interviewee answer it. You may hear about company strengths that aren't being sufficiently supported or celebrated. You'll also learn about group and individual perceptions regarding the company's best attributes.

5. **What isn't working?** This broad question can tell you a great deal about company problems and about individual and group perceptions.

6. **What do you want to be famous for?** Richard Andersen, president and CEO of Northlands in Edmonton, Alberta, has asked this question as part of the snapshot process every time he moves to a new job. The query is designed to ferret out colleagues' goals and aspirations. Ambitious answers can reveal the degree to which someone hopes to rise in the company, as well as that person's vision, creativity, and problem-solving capacity. Uncomfortable responses also tell you something about the company. Organizations that are not good at dreaming are not very good at creating, either.

7. **Describe progress made on important goals or projects in the company, and identify challenges and responsibilities.** This final step in the interview process calls for a presentation. The goal of the presentation step is to help you understand the nitty-gritty daily work of the organization: What is the business of this business? You will gain perspective on important company issues and learn the degree of clarity interviewees have about how their own work fits into organizational goals.

Remember, the length of each interview, and this final step in particular, will vary according to the complexity of each person's job. You might organize this part of the process collaboratively. If several people work closely on a particular project, it may be easier for them to make a presentation on this final question together. Don't get so many people involved, though, that you can't assess each worker's presentation skills and ask individual questions. What you learn about the people you work with is as important as what you learn about the work.

Reflect on the Introductory Interviews

Don't assume that your openness to communication and collaboration will automatically mean that constituents can offer articulate expositions of what they do and how their work connects with the company's overarching mission. Not everyone is so insightful.

Don't assume that the introductory interviews will directly lead to organizational happiness, either. If you've been brought in to make significant changes to a company working below its capacities, this dialogue will likely uncover emotional sore points, disconnects, and confusion. Some of the topics you uncover may not have been addressed in years, though they should have been. Now you're here, pulling back the covers and shining a spotlight on the problems. Ultimately, this is a necessary part of the learning process.

These interviews won't necessarily solve the most difficult challenges that lie ahead. Fortunate leaders may be able to stimulate immediate, positive changes simply by igniting the conversation, but that won't be true for every leader at every organization. Don't be discouraged if this process stirs emotions and leaves everyone with more questions than answers. This level of emotional engagement is necessary to stimulate the deepest levels of individual and collective learning. The deeper the problems, the more you may have to dig during the snapshot process to begin unearthing them.

Consider organizing interviewer responses and your thoughts on a grid like the one in the graphic.

The Job They Say You Have	The Job You Do	The Job You Should Be Doing	Disconnect	Reflection

Lay out your notes this way, and you'll quickly see disconnects. For example, after doing ten snapshot interviews, your chart may show a consistent disconnect between the jobs people were given and the jobs they are actually doing. Maybe the jobs changed, but the system never adjusted. Maybe leaders never had conversations, so jobs just sort of evolved. A major disconnect between the jobs people do and the jobs they should be doing could be due to overly rigid administrative practices, or to a lack of communication between groups. Whatever the cause, analyzing the patterns you see can help you move forward. In the next chapter, we'll discuss how to analyze other information from the introductory interviews, in particular what mental models the interviews reveal.

Key Terms

Snapshot interview

Job description

Job responsibilities

Presentation

Questions for Reflection

1. What can I learn from my constituents' presentations about the current state of their job responsibilities?

2. What actions can I take to a resolve disconnects between the jobs being done and the jobs that should be done?

3. How could an observer help me reflect on my snapshot interviews? What insights might someone help me gain?

Chapter 5

Matching Mental Models

PEOPLE—INCLUDING LEADERS—OFTEN unconsciously believe that everyone sees the world the way they do. In fact, the exact opposite is likely true. Our work environments are much more diverse than ever before, so leaders must assume that their constituents have had a great variety of experiences. Diversity in age, experience, religion, culture, and background means that the world one person sees at work is not the same world that colleagues see. These different perspectives, or *mental models*, have a significant effect on the steps a leader takes to influence change. Leaders must take into account variances in perspective if they are to create a significant leadership impact.

Since mental models profoundly influence how we see the world, it is difficult to build a truly connected culture if we don't take the time to examine the similarities and differences in our prevailing—and controlling—mental models. Furthermore, we can more quickly articulate a learning agenda if we first establish some clarity about our current mental models and what they mean to us.

In phase 2 of your first 100 days, you will continue to develop your understanding of the individual and collective work going on in your organization by examining how mental models shape that work. Having conducted formal interviews in step 1 of the snapshot process, you will now gather information informally. You will use your formal and informal observations in step 2 of the snapshot process, discussed in the next chapter.

The 100-Day Timeline

Phase 1: Days 1–6	Phase 2: Days 7–39	Phase 3: Days 40–69	Phase 4: Days 70–100
Creating a Lasting First Impression	Getting in Motion	Testing and Trusting	Celebrating and Looking Forward

The Learning Power of Diversity

Darlene is a new division leader in a company that makes nutritional supplements and skin and beauty aids. Although she is responsible for a larger workforce, she has an immediate team of five with whom she will work regularly.

Jack is 55, originally from Texas and a proud graduate of Abilene Christian University. He has been with the company for seventeen years and is a grandfather of three. Known for his ready smile and affable disposition, he is always there to lend a guiding hand and is adroit at bringing great levels of energy to everything he does. He struggles a bit with new technology, but his collaborative skills are so strong that he rarely has trouble meeting deadlines.

Dave is 41, an African American Muslim from Los Angeles. He has been with the company for seven years. Dave is comfortable with new technology but struggles with some software applications and with the concept of systems thinking. He is friendly and willing to work with others, but like others with his learning style, he prefers to work alone. Dave has a quiet ability to patiently solve problems and bring unique solutions when others have had a difficult time. Although he studied at Grambling University in the South, his heart is in California.

Kate is 31 and has lived in the United States for two years. All of her education and previous work experience were in India, where she is from. Kate is known as a quiet problem solver and is extremely warm. She is adroit at using technology and data and frequently advocates for meta-analysis as a mechanism for solving problems.

Pam is 32. She lived in rural Alaska until five years ago. A proud vegan, she is a vocal advocate for animal rights and gay and lesbian issues. She and her life partner have a new baby. Confident and energetic, Pam takes an application-oriented approach to using technology. On most days she can keep up with Brian and Kate.

Brian is 28 and is from Boston. He was educated at Harvard and is proudly single. In eighteen months at the company he has risen fast. Known for his boyish charm and his affinity for video games, he successfully applies technology and has been exposed to some of the world's top business scholars. His ability to use social networking spaces lets him connect with people all over the world who can lend a hand when his team is in trouble.

While doing her morning yoga before heading in to work, Darlene quietly meditates on the leadership challenges she faces in the days and weeks to come. She smiles to herself as she thinks about just how diverse this particular team happened to be. She remembers a time early in her career, when dealing with diversity was seen as a kind of necessary evil—when employers struggled to get people from widely divergent perspectives to work together and try to move forward as one. Darlene, however, has learned firsthand the unbelievable advantage gained by working with a talented and wildly diverse team. She has no doubt that Jack, Dave, Kate, Brian, and Pam will present varied perspectives on each issue thanks to their unique backgrounds, interests, skills, and personal pursuits. She knows that her team will bring diverse mental models to every challenge they face; if she engenders the right type of leadership impact, unprecedented levels of creativity and innovation are likely to emerge. As she stretches, she wonders, however, whether her team values that diversity. Does the team have creative friction, or just friction? Do they appreciate the rich diversity within the team, or denigrate their differences as too polarizing?

One of the reasons that job descriptions and explicit systemic hierarchies are difficult to apply in many companies today is the fluidity of the work itself. Not every project is tailor-made for the same leader to provide the same type of leadership. A new work challenge may place unique demands on a team that suddenly make the leadership of a particular team member far more important than it has been in the past. Darlene has a very diverse team; her leadership could be measured in part by her ability to create an environment in which the best leader can emerge at any time given the challenge at hand.

Exploring Mental Models

A mental model is a prism through which we see the world.[1] Mental models are our ideas and associations around a particular thing. For example, if as a young child you went to the circus and were nearly trampled by an elephant, your initial perception of the circus experience would be negative. As a result, you might develop negative mental models about circuses, live entertainment, pachyderms—perhaps all African mammals, for that matter—and be highly reluctant to go to a zoo.

Our mental models are based on our experiences and how we reflect on them over time. Only direct experience can show us a person's mental models. Even though we know a little bit about Darlene's team, we can't make assumptions about who they are or the mental models they carry. Leaders should directly examine mental models, identify consistencies and inconsistencies, and consider how these models may affect the organization's work and the hoped-for leadership impact.

You may find that your team doesn't see success, reform, or transformation as even possible in their work. In their mental models the company may be in gridlock, or surrounded by challenges so great that there is no possibility of change. All your leadership will mean very little if you don't challenge defeatist mental models.

Finding the Prevailing Mental Models

Mental models are perceptions, also called *mental frames*, that individuals have about key organizational concepts. Every person and organization has them. Employees' mental models about their work or themselves can, to a great extent, shape their emotions and actions. Mental models are entirely personal. Even so, groups that work together for a while can develop *collective* mental models about particular issues.

The more adroitly you identify your organization's individual and group mental models, the more quickly you will understand how to create a meaningful leadership impact. As you spend time walking through the organization and talking with people, focus on discovering their individual and collective mental models.

Individuals and groups typically have mental models in the following nine categories:

1. **Leadership.** As we've discussed, there's a big difference between seeing a *leader* as the person who makes all the decisions and seeing *leadership* as an emergent force that can reshape an organization. As you chat with your new colleagues, take note of how they view these concepts. Do they see leadership as something of which they are a part? Try to get this information before you talk too much about your own leadership preferences, so the answers aren't just a version of what people think you want to hear.

2. **Learning and professional development.** Without exception, your colleagues need to continue developing their capacity to learn new things. Work to understand the individual and prevailing collective mental models regarding formal or informal learning and professional development. Are people excited about learning new things, or do they feel dread as they anticipate a flood of new expectations?

3. **Change.** Do your constituents see change as being done to them, or as emanating from them? If difficult market conditions have had a significant impact on their work, encourage colleagues to at least control their own reactions to these challenges.

4. **Customers.** How often do you hear talk about customers? Can workers visualize the customer? How would you gauge their emotional reaction to that question?

5. **Service.** One way or another, everyone is in the service business. Do you sense a service orientation at your organization? Some might argue that organizations either exist to be served or to serve others. Those that exist to be served generally do not add as much value as those that exist to serve.

6. **The company or organization.** What do people think about the company? Do they speak of it with fondness and love? Do they acknowledge good intentions, despite the inevitable fumbles? Or

do they have cold, corporate tones in their voices when they talk about the organization?

7. **Their jobs.** How do workers talk about their jobs? Are they enthusiastic about what they do? Do they want to teach you about it? Do they talk about the art of possibility and emerging opportunities?

8. **The past, present, and future.** What words and tone do people use as they describe the company's past, present, and future? Do they focus on one time to the exclusion of others, for example, talking at great length about the past but hardly mentioning the future? The most productive groups know and acknowledge the past, reflect on the present, and talk with clarity and decisiveness about the future they hope to create.

9. **The competition.** Does your team respect their competitors? Do they acknowledge the competition's strengths and consider ways your company might keep or take the lead?

Ask Key Questions

In chapter 4, I introduced the snapshot process and provided some formative questions to use in your introductory interviews to ascertain how individual team members see their jobs and how they comprehend change and improvement in the organization. Now I will introduce some additional concepts to explore in informal conversations to prepare for step 2, sharing findings and goal setting. Before you can set goals, you must discover some of the essential mental models that drive the work of each of the team members you work with most directly.

We know that the development of a connected community and real learning power has a lot to do with how team members see themselves, their work, and each other. If the collective mental model has established limitations on the team's learning potential, it will be difficult to achieve new goals. By better understanding those mental models before goal setting, you improve your ability to address hidden barriers and deepen your leadership impact.

The kinds of questions to ask are those that relate directly to change and continuous improvement. Present the questions in two ways (you may not have the opportunity to explore them all): first, try to solicit the person's opinion directly. Next, ask the respondent to share how others might answer the question. The advantage of this second approach is that researchers have found that we are often more honest about our feelings when describing them in terms of how others might feel.[2] Political polls, for example, often handicap elections by asking the head of household in a telephone survey who their neighbors are likely to vote for. This usually elicits the most honest response.

Ask questions such as the following:

- Where do you think leadership originates in this organization? Where do others think leadership originates?

- How does this organization facilitate learning on the job? How would the group answer this question?

- How do you contribute to change? How do others think you contribute to change?

- How do you think change happens in this organization? How do others think change happens?

- Who are our customers? What do you do for them?

- What service do you provide? What service do others think you provide?

- How would you characterize this company? How would your peers characterize it?

- How would you describe your job? How would others describe it?

- How do you see the company's future? How does the group see the company's future?

- How would you characterize the company's past? How would others characterize the company's past?

- How do you see the firm's present? How would others answer the same question?

- How do you imagine the future? How do your coworkers imagine the future?

- How would you characterize the competition? How would others characterize the competition?

Reflect on Mental Models

Take notes in any way that makes sense to you, and consider condensing what you've captured into summaries. A chart such this one may be helpful.

My Mental Model	Staff Mental Model	Similarities	Tensions	Reflections

It's important to jot notes on your own mental model for each item. You may not know everything about the company yet, but you certainly have a perspective on leadership, learning, change, the firm's customers, its service, and so on. A comparison between your models and existing individual and collective models will show similarities and tensions, helping you better understand the challenges or opportunities that lie ahead. This exercise may also help you compare team members' individual mental models. You'll begin to see the diversity of thinking on your team and the degree to which colleagues' similarities or differences may shape the group. In step 2 of the snapshot process you'll have opportunities to talk with your team about the similarities and differences you've found.

You may find that your colleagues have dramatically different mental models. That can be both beneficial and healthy. Someone in a leadership position, for example, is often expected to promote greater degrees of out-of-the-box thinking and creativity. With an effective leader, a team with members who have had a wide variety of experiences will help the company reach more creative levels of innovation.

Changing Mental Models

You may find disempowering mental models deeply entrenched in your new organization. Can you change these individual and collective perceptions?

Changing mental models is tricky business. A person's initial exposure to a new concept typically forms a mental model around that concept. Every subsequent exposure to that concept happens in direct relation to the initial mental model.[3] Once negative mental models are set, they can be very difficult to "unlearn."

Even so, rerouting mental models is possible—with work and care. The following seven steps can help you work with your constituents to build new, more positive mental models.

Have a Critical Conversation

If your team historically has a negative view of competition, change, or some other key organizational element, have a thoughtful discussion about the need to find a new way of seeing this concept. Examples of instances in which negative views have come up during critical conversations can help emphasize the need for change.

These conversations may be with individuals or with groups. With Darlene's team, imagine how different her individual critical conversations would be with Jack, the 55-year-old graduate of Abilene Christian University, versus Brian, the 28-year-old Boston-born Harvard graduate. Without having the critical conversation, however, Darlene can't necessarily predict how Jack, Brian, or any other member of her team will respond to a certain topic that might be important to her. Having these critical conversations collaboratively helps the team get to know each other's perspectives and helps Darlene clarify what role might be most important for her in leading the team.

Many well-intended leaders stop after this step. They use words to address a disempowering perception, hoping that constituents will begin to reflect differently on their experiences. Some action-oriented individuals and teams might be proactive enough to change based on a conversation. For many others, though, additional steps are necessary.

Construct a Focused New Model

Reconstructing a mental model requires thoughtful conversation about what the new mental model should be. For example, a team that consistently views leadership purely in a position-oriented way might need to have an extended conversation about the potential benefits of seeing leadership as a more organic, free-flowing force available throughout the organization. How might a new mental model affect actions taken throughout the organization? Would a new mental model affect team interactions? Would it affect how employees see the change process? Would it affect accountability?

Focus on exactly how a new mental model would impact daily operations and each person's work. This reconstruction process makes a new mental model real and lets participants actively reflect on what's possible.

If Darlene has her entire team work together on this construction process, she certainly would have a wide variety of collective experiences to draw upon. When trying to visualize the possibilities, Dave, the Los Angeles–born digital immigrant, could certainly collaborate with application-oriented Pam to articulate an entirely new vision. Pam's energy and enthusiasm will complement Dave's patience and focus.

Compare Old and New Mental Models

Don't ignore past mental models. Purposefully *compare* old and new perceptions. For example, as you talk about leadership by position versus leadership as available to everyone within an organization, a thoughtful comparison between the old and new models helps constituents examine and challenge their original perceptions.

Darlene could have an extremely enlightening conversation with her team in comparing old and new mental models in relationship to their work together. Even though the team might have had the same collective experiences at the company, their individual backgrounds will likely create differing perspectives on the existing old mental models and the emerging new mental models. Thoughtfully reflecting individually and collectively on these concepts could drive home Darlene's leadership impact.

Use the Power of Emotion

Emotion is the key to learning. Mental models initially form in reaction to emotionally resonant, memorable experiences. Just being exposed to something doesn't mean you have a mental model about it. You've had experiences—driving over asphalt, for instance—that haven't resulted in mental models because the events weren't emotional for you. Mental models require emotional associations.

Constructing a new mental model means making a new emotional association.[4] Emotions such as curiosity, courage, and determination might all be associations for a new mental model of leadership, for example. Don't shy away from emotionally bound conversations around new mental models. Emotion drives engagement. Use emotions thoughtfully and productively to help reconstruct an old mental model.

In examining mental models, it is important not to typecast certain mental models as aligning with particular personal characteristics. A quiet person, for example, doesn't necessarily lack passion for excellence. Kate, the 31-year-old Indian who has only been in the United States for two years, has emerged as a quiet problem solver on Darlene's team and may appear to work with a certain reserve. Darlene shouldn't assume that Kate's demeanor signals a lack of emotion or a disconnect with the team or company. Kate may have deep emotional connections to her work and may demonstrate her passionate pursuit of excellence differently than exuberant teammates like Jack.

Regardless of how each individual expresses emotion, when leaders are willing to be thoughtful about emotional engagement, positive and impactful emotional states are more likely to emerge. The ability to conjure up, manage, and facilitate emotional energy will go a long way in shaping positive new collective mental models.

Use the Power of Action

Our brains pay attention to what we say and how we say it, but they pay even more attention to the actions we take. We might talk about how important it is to be fit, but our brains (and our bodies) take much more notice if we actually exercise.

To reconfigure a mental model, then, it's important to walk the walk—not just talk the talk. If you want people to think of leadership as something that's available to anyone, take immediate steps to make sure that leading really is something anyone at your company can do.

In Darlene's case, she and her teammates will need to give thoughtful consideration to the immediate actions they can take to reinforce their new mental models. If, for example, Darlene is attempting to create a new mental model in relationship to work quality, it may benefit her team to commit to specific, immediate actions that will reinforce that model. When the new mental model is thoughtfully constructed and tied to specific actions, it gains momentum throughout the organization.

Practice, Practice, Practice

The first five steps often take place in training sessions. But once people return to their regular routines, it's easy for old habits to take over. Consistent practice is an important step in constructing a new mental model that really sticks.

Perhaps you'd like your constituents to see leadership as a more organic force in the organization—one that results in more collaboration, ownership, and localized action. Build opportunities for them to practice collaboration. Give them chances to take action and demonstrate ownership. Consistent practice helps reinforce the new vision.

As the leader, Darlene's role is to ensure that practice happens: to reiterate the commitment to practice in every formal meeting and to search for evidence that it's actually happening in her informal observations.

Consistently Revisit New Mental Models

Getting off track is easy. Leaders should consistently revisit and clarify the new mental model whenever possible. At this stage, it's critical to draw attention to what the desired mental model looks like in action: where the team has made changes that reflect the new mental model, where they've made changes that don't work, and where they have yet to make the needed changes.

If Darlene's team is advancing a more deliberate notion of what quality means, then, it is important that she revisit that model early and often to ensure that, in fact, everyone understands the new model in the same way and is operating accordingly. Suppose Brian interpreted the drive toward quality as a signal to dramatically raise work expectations; he may have started confronting people throughout the organization for not meeting the new proposed standard of excellence. If confrontation was the agreed-upon notion of how excellence was to be observed and established, then Brian would be on safe ground. But perhaps issuing challenges day after day wasn't at all what the team had in mind; without mindful and consistent conversation, Brian's inappropriate strategy for reinforcing the mental model might continue. Darlene and the team must continually articulate their assumptions regarding how the new mental model will be promoted and measured.

Key Terms

Individual and collective mental models

Diversity

Critical conversation

Power of emotion

Change

Practice

Questions for Reflection

1. Are there significant differences between my constituents' mental models for the group, company, or organization? What does this say about my leadership challenges?

2. Did my constituents struggle to explain their mental models? Were they clear about their perceptions?

3. Overall, were there significant disagreements between my mental models and those of my team? What might this mean to me as a leader?

Chapter 6

Building a Better Vision

THE WORD *vision* CROPS up all over the business world, especially in books about leadership change or organizational development. You'll both pose and field questions about your vision for the company from constituents, boards of directors, shareholders, fellow managers, and superiors. As you listen, compare their responses with your own leadership sensibilities. Their vision, your vision, a collective vision—which one is the right vision?

It's not easy to develop an action-ready leadership vision. The process gets easier when you understand the power of vision in a way that's application oriented—not theoretical.

The 100-Day Timeline

Phase 1: Days 1–6	Phase 2: Days 7–39	Phase 3: Days 40–69	Phase 4: Days 70–100
Creating a Lasting First Impression	Getting in Motion	Testing and Trusting	Celebrating and Looking Forward

A leader's vision is revealed during every phase and every step of the snapshot process. You begin making an impact in phase 1: in your first week on the job, employees and peers will develop opinions about your vision and start to evaluate your capacity to advance and sustain that vision. You've investigated current mental models, and perhaps started a process to create a new, more positive collective mental model. In phase 2, you will learn strategies to clarify a new vision of what is possible and to harness mental models to fulfill that vision.

Turning Around, or Going in Circles?

Cam was silent at dinner. Debbie, his wife of twenty years, knew that when Cam was struggling at work, he got quiet and spent time at dinner thinking through the challenges of his day. By dessert, he was usually ready to talk.

Cam had recently been promoted to be the new manager at the biggest, most profitable branch of a large, family-owned department store in a small town in the deep South. The company had been in town for almost 100 years. The original owners were firmly entrenched figures in the community. They were known throughout the state for their generous contributions to city charities and schools.

In the last several years, however, store profits had begun to slide. There were no outward signs that things were turning sour, but Cam had seen the books. Customers had discovered lower Internet prices on items they would otherwise have purchased in town.

Cam had his work cut out for him. He was frustrated, though, that he couldn't get ownership to articulate what exactly they wanted from him as a manager. "They brought me in to get them out of this downward spiral, but I just can't get a handle on their vision for turning things around," Cam told his wife. "When I came in, I presented some ideas that I thought would quickly help turn the store around. I got a lot of resistance from division managers and from family relatives who work in the store. They all seemed to be concerned that we are somehow moving away from the original concepts behind the store. They are losing money every month, and the pathway forward is so clear. I don't understand the resistance."

Debbie allowed a few moments to pass before she spoke. "It sounds to me like you see the store's problems quite clearly. Do you think everyone around you is seeing the same thing?"

Businesses want leaders with vision. However, leaders are never particularly clear about whether their vision aligns with those around them. In Cam's case, conflicting visions for what the department store was and what it could be were creating confusion. The family ownership team had a vision steeped in history and tradition. Many of the veteran managers also were operating from older paradigms. Cam, on the other hand, saw the current situation and understood that the strategies that brought success in the past may not lead to success in the future.

Maybe Cam has all the right ideas and is being stifled by deeply entrenched business patterns. Or maybe the store would find only peril by neglecting its past, as has happened to other businesses. Sometimes these entrenched patterns get that way for a very good reason: they work! Cam's suggestions might move the store even further from the hometown atmosphere that made it famous, maybe moving customers even faster toward online shopping. Whether the vision for the company changes a little or a lot, it's essential that the leader find a common vision that will connect culture throughout the organization and provide a focus for developing learning power.

Understanding Vision Components

It's difficult to develop a vision on which everyone can agree. There are strategies, however, that can make the process easier and more successful. First, let's examine the components that affect the way we develop a vision.

History

The longer we're alive, the more directly history plays into our ability to establish a vision.[1] For example, if your friend of twenty years has been a key companion through good times and bad, your emotionally bound experience creates a history that affects your view of that person and your thoughts when you hear that friend mentioned. You might be much more excited, for example, to accept an invitation to lunch with a group of friends if this person were also invited. The lunch you envision would inevitably involve your feelings about your friend.

The department store's history as a stalwart, brick-and-mortar part of the community will likewise affect Cam's vision for the company's future. The company's past doesn't mean it can't follow a dramatically different vision for its future. In this case, though, the history presents a challenge that can't be ignored if the company does dramatically change its vision.

Mental Models

Learning theory also tells us that mental models are an important consideration in developing an individual or collective vision. Consider the previous example: an invitation to lunch with friends. Your mental models around this experience would include categorized perceptions of luncheons in your town, anticipated food, and the social activities that might accompany this experience. If instead of lunch you were meeting friends for drinks on a Friday after work, your mental model of the potential experience would likely be different, even if you planned to go with the same people.

History is often local, but our mental models travel with us. Cam has mental models about how a successful, contemporary store should operate. He would likely have the same perceptions if he worked for another business in a different community.

Current Context

Situational contexts affect our mental models. Perhaps your friend has been sick, so you envision asking after her health. Or maybe you and your friend have had an argument, so you are a bit apprehensive about lunch or picture yourself apologizing over the soup.

Putting It All Together

There is no exact science in terms of how our history, mental models, and current context all come together to create a vision. It depends, to a great extent, on the new ideas being considered, the relative experience level of the individual constructing a vision, and a myriad of other factors that may emerge simultaneously. Let's consider an example of how vision is constructed at the workplace and take a look at how the entire process can ebb and flow between consideration of history, mental models, and context.

Imagine a team with 10 members. Five of them are younger than 35 and are extremely comfortable with technology (the part of the demographic often referred to as *digital natives*). The five other members are older than 55 and struggle with some of the company's emerging technological demands; they are *digital immigrants.*[2]

Each member of the team receives a state-of-the-art netbook and a smartphone. These tools will let them do all of their reporting on the move and replace their old desktop and laptop computers.

Let's consider the different ways that team members might imagine their new situation in light of the factors that affect vision:

- **History.** The younger team members probably grew up using technology regularly and can't remember a time when they didn't use it. The older digital immigrants may have had various degrees of success in using technology and certainly remember life before computers became household items.

- **Mental models.** For digital natives, the new equipment is just another example of how technology makes life easier. Digital immigrants might see the new tools as something frustrating that interrupts their preferred ways of working, or as yet another thing to learn in an already full workday.

- **Current context.** Both groups may share a collective recognition that the team needs cutting-edge technology to stay competitive. But while half of the team may see these tools as the key to greater levels of work ease, efficiency, and effectiveness, the other half might imagine increased frustration levels, hindrances, and lots of mistakes. A leader who assumes that the entire team sees the same thing when they talk about technological change would be sadly mistaken.

Effective leaders must recognize that every constituent has a unique history, has built unknown mental models, and may not agree with colleagues about the current context. Yet there is the team, a group of people who have to work together. When you think about how complex it is to construct a vision, even when these concepts are aligned, it is amazing that anyone ever develops a connected vision at all.

How can leader effectively use what they know about the vision construction process? The answer lies in how you share the snapshot you've taken of the company during introductory interviews and how you use what you've learned to create a new collective vision of the future.

Step 2: Sharing Findings and Goal Setting

You are now in step 2 of the snapshot process. In step 1, you gathered information and learned as much as you could from those you will be leading as you move forward. Now you will begin the process of sharing what you heard and your perceptions, and creating opportunities to clarify the vision, set some goals, and gain momentum. This is a key step in deepening your leadership impact.

Early in phase 2, by day 10 or so, depending on your organization's size and complexity, call a final meeting including all your snapshot interviewees. Though this meeting will have interactive elements, you'll do much of the talking, telling your team what you heard in the snapshot interviews and how you've interpreted it.

Maximize engagement by keeping the meeting short. Don't get bogged down in minutia. Instead, work to capture the main issues you've identified in relationship to history, key mental models, and the current situational context. By doing so, you use a single meeting to share a snapshot of where the organization, company, or division stands today, and you show the group all the moving parts necessary to constructing a vision. This overview is of great practical value and helps your team build confidence in you as a leader. The more organized your presentation, the better. Consider creating handouts that cover your main points.

When you've finished your presentation, ask your team some important questions. For example:

- If we were able to manage situational variables, came together around the mental models that help shape our work, and kept our history in perspective, what kind of new and better outcomes could we achieve?

- What's possible for us as a company, a team, a division?

Because the group has just discussed the history, key mental models, and current situational context, this is a perfect moment for the team to begin articulating a new vision that is clear to everybody in the room.

Capture as much of this important meeting as you can in your notes. Remember, though, that the power of a vision lies in how that vision becomes action. Before ending the meeting, identify a key goal or several goals (not too many!) that could be accomplished in the next 90 days and would bring the organization forward in an important and, perhaps, momentum-building way. These 90-day goals should be few in number, rigorous but actionable, and chosen in direct relationship to the vision the team is beginning to establish.

Picking a 90-day goal offers several advantages. The team leaves the meeting with some clarity about your shared vision and a plan to work toward that vision. A relatively short-term goal lets the team take action *now* without being overly committed to a vision that may evolve in the weeks and months to come. The team gives itself the opportunity to go back and reflect on what was discussed. A group can't come to absolute clarity about a vision in just one meeting, though this initial snapshot discussion is powerful. You'll have at least two progress checks later and will likely see evolving clarity about how the team sees its work and the direction the company needs to go.

The Vision and Its Learning Impact

You've seen how a leader and team can strategically construct a vision. Think about how the factors that affect vision building will affect you and your ability to create a leadership impact, build a more connected culture, and enhance organizational learning power.

Consider your organization's history. How connected and comfortable have constituents been in the past? Do most of the people who work in your organization feel comfortable and connected with their colleagues and with the company's objectives? If not, that disconnect will be a key mental model for you to overcome.

Think about the history of learning in the company. Do your constituents value learning? Can they articulate their learning objectives? Are they aware of their own learning strengths? Are there negative feelings about professional development, or does the team see connecting and learning as powerful tools that make them more effective (and more human)?

Next, reflect on existing mental models around connection and learning. Does your team see collaboration as a requirement, or as something that's pleasurable and leads to better outcomes? Finally, how do team members see their current working situations in relation to connection and learning? Being aware of these issues can help you develop a more powerful leadership impact.

Vision, Performance, and Results

You've learned about mental models and vision, and how they are influenced by history, mental models, and current context. Use these concepts to discuss and analyze how your constituents view their performances and results. What explicit visions do they have for their own performances and the results they hope to achieve? In leading this conversation, consider asking your team to reflect on history and current context, and then to identify key mental models about their own performances and results. If you hope to help your firm improve performance and change results, the ways you visualize them are extremely important.

Key Terms

Vision

History

Mental models

Current context

90-day goals

Performance and results

Questions for Reflection

1. During step 2 of the snapshot process, what significant piece of history did I learn about? How does this history shape my leadership approach?

2. Of the mental models I learned about during step 2 of the snapshot process, which will have the most effect on my role as a leader?

3. What have I learned about the current context of my organization? How has that shaped my perspectives?

Chapter 7

Testing and Trusting

COMIC BOOKS AND MOVIES often portray heroes as fearless. In the real world, however, fear is an important mitigating emotion for even the bravest leader. A fearless leader might even be dangerous, with a tendency to push organizations into untenable circumstances and unnecessary levels of danger and pain. A courageous leader, on the other hand, is one who can think through priorities and address difficult challenges.

Effective leaders remember, especially in their first 100 days, that fear is a natural aspect of human experience and will always have an impact on how we lead and how others respond to us. Instead of fighting fear, leaders should work to understand how individual and collective fear and stress work, acknowledging its effects on the transition process. Getting over the initial fear and apprehension associated with new leadership involves a natural process of testing, one that ideally ends in acceptance and trusting.

You are now in phase 3 of your first 100 days. You have been on the job for at least 40 days, and the institution is beginning to comprehend what your leadership impact will be. Now is also the time, however, when constituents may begin to wonder if there is truth in your advertising. As a leader, do you really mean what you say? Do you walk the talk?

In this chapter you will learn how this important testing and trusting process ultimately impacts the degree to which your team embraces and understands the leadership impact you are trying to develop. In order to build a more connected culture with opportunities for real learning power to emerge, the system has to trust that the leader's positions and priorities have durability.

This is also the phase when you will begin to test and trust the organization: to carefully examine what has developed thus far and to observe the degree to which the thoughts, ideas, visions, and aspirations others espoused earlier in your first 100 days are truly consistent with their actions on a daily basis. Testing, trusting, observing, and reflecting are critical checkpoints in the process of making a leadership impact. In this chapter, we'll discuss the informal testing and trusting you'll experience; in the next, we'll examine how to formalize testing and trusting into progress checks in step 3 and 4 of the snapshot process.

The 100-Day Timeline

Phase 1: Days 1–6	Phase 2: Days 7–39	Phase 3: Days 40–69	Phase 4: Days 70–100
Creating a Lasting First Impression	Getting in Motion	Testing and Trusting	Celebrating and Looking Forward

Tight-Lipped

Jon remembers well his second interview with "old man Whitaker," as his new employer introduced himself. "Thirty years ago, when this company was Whitaker Snowing and Towing, I had just one truck with a tow hitch on the back and a snowblade on the front," Mr. Whitaker told Jon that day. "I worked in the morning plowing streets and parking lots and then drove all day pulling people out of ditches. Those were the fun days!"

Today, Mr. Whitaker owns the largest privately owned snow removal business in the Midwest. He has contracts in border regions in three states and has developed a competitive business that, in addition to private snow removal work, takes on government contracts when they were made available. Due to some changes in state regulations, Mr. Whitaker's company has some unique growth opportunities ahead, in the government sector in particular. As the new vice president, however, Jon knows that to win these new government bids, a number of things about how the business is organized and executes its work will have to change.

Despite the changes and challenges ahead, Jon is enthusiastic about his new management position. He looked forward to meeting the 25 people who report to him and to begin making progress on the changes that will help the company move forward and thrive.

When Jon met his team, however, he was surprised at how little they were willing to share about their thoughts regarding the company. When he asked one of the managers, "So, tell me one of your goals for the company," the manager gave a formal response that sounded more like a canned mission statement than any heartfelt vision for the company.

As Jon reflected later on the conversations he had with various constituents, he was puzzled by what he described to his friends as an "eerie silence" that seemed to permeate the institution. His staff was polite, obedient, and responsive, but they didn't seem very interested in sharing their thoughts, ideas, and aspirations—about anything.

Jon knew that his division wasn't as productive as it could be and that changes were needed if these new contracts were indeed going to be won and executed. He would have to break this code of silence and establish an improved level of trust and understanding if he was to succeed in making an impact. This tight-lipped, rather nervous organizational culture hadn't yielded much innovation in many years. Jon recognized that this, too, had to change, and that it was his job as a leader to create a new culture that would embrace the challenges ahead.

Many leaders move into working environments where a nearly palpable fear and uncertainty have a stranglehold on the institution. In this chapter, we will talk about fear and the institutional reality that all new leaders are tested to some degree. Testing serves as a way to learn a new leader's management style; it also establishes the degree to which constituents can trust a new leader. Understanding and prospering in the testing period is essential for leadership success.

What Is Fear, and What Does It Do?

In almost every work environment, people talk about feelings of stress or anxiety. Psychologists disagree on the number of actual emotions we experience and our ability to express a nuanced difference between one emotion and another, but many of our negative or uncomfortable emotions relate to fear.[1] For the purposes of this text, and for your work as a practitioner, you should know a couple of essential things about managing fear.

First, fear can never be eliminated from human experience. Even in extremely comfortable surroundings, our brains scan the environment for danger.[2] This is how our species survives, and fear doesn't have an off switch. No amount of connection and learning power will prevent your team from running for cover, for instance, if the walls literally fall in.

Second, our ancestors felt and responded to fear in ways that allowed them to survive and reproduce. That's the only reason you're reading this book. With each new generation, we get better and better at responding to fear. Everyone has fears that can be triggered at any given time.

Our brains cannot distinguish between animal fear and psychological fear (Wolfe, 2001). When we fear missing a deadline, our brains physiologically respond in exactly the same way they would if we were in danger of being eaten by a bear. In the ideal real world, of course, a missed deadline would be much less dangerous—and emotionally draining—than being eaten by a wild animal. Our emotions don't recognize that.

Fear stops learning in its tracks.[3] It's impossible to learn when the brain is distracted by fear—a rule that's especially true when the new material is rigorous. Teachers and principals working in tough urban environments often have difficulty facilitating the deepest learning levels. Their social environments are so toxic that students' brains are literally shut off from deep learning, focused instead on either psychological or animal fear.

The same is true in toxic organizations. Companies that have fired many people or created frequent, stressful situations build an environment of toxicity and fear that shuts down the organization's most creative aspects. When competition threatens your firm's very existence, your team's fear of being fired or outsourced is exactly the emotional mindset that will prevent the innovation and improvement that would get the team out of trouble.

In toxic environments, successful leaders find ways to disengage fear and help workers grow and learn at their creative bests.

Fear and Change

It's natural to fear change, particularly when the change is from the known to the unknown. Evolution doesn't typically favor the first person who goes into a dark cave. When change occurs at work, most of us quietly question whether the adjustment will push us to the point of incompetence, irrelevance, or both. Any change to comfortable professional circumstances is a potential challenge to our well-fed status quo.

A new leader brings uncertainty. Until that uncertainty is quelled, fear may be an important part of how your constituents interact with you. Even if your predecessor was not particularly well liked, most people still prefer a known negative to an unknown novelty. Even if everyone is glad to have a new leader in place, they may still worry that you will decide that a certain job function or a particular individual or team is no longer relevant to the company's needs.

Some team members may experience a lot of anxiety in response to change. Maybe they suspect that their job functions are inessential, or perhaps they're just anxious people. Others may feel comparatively minor stress. These people might have been part of your interview process, met you many times, or had particularly pleasant interactions with you. These experiences can generate a great deal of hope and excitement about the possibilities that lie ahead.

Testing the Leader

All organizations put leaders through a testing process. Your response to this process determines the degree to which your constituents will trust you.

Though it may not feel good to experience that testing, the testing process is ultimately very helpful. Organizations need to know the merits of those who are in a position to have a profound impact on the system's daily direction and progress. The testing process helps to identify leaders' strong suits and limitations.

When you were in school, your instructors used tests to assess your competence in a particular area. As a leader in your first 100 days, you'll be tested at various points and in different ways. Some of these tests will look like the ones you took in school. Others may come in different forms, with tests sometimes under way without your knowledge. To gain your team's trust and cooperation, it's important that you consider in advance how you'll respond.

Pop Quizzes

All new leaders face pop quizzes during their first 100 days. (These quizzes are especially common in toxic work environments.) It's hard to prepare for these quizzes, because they surface in a completely extemporaneous way. Maybe some constituents are particularly concerned to know your opinion of a specific aspect of their job function. Out of the blue, one might ask you a very pointed, specific, public question about your philosophy or perspective. These uncomfortable moments can be important in building trust—but only if you answer the questions as honestly and consistently as you possibly can.

At the snow removal company discussed earlier, Jon might face a pop quiz like this: "If one of us comes to you with an idea for change that has cost implications, are you willing to go to Mr. Whitaker to get funding to make the change possible?"

Before we discuss Jon's response, think about this. The individual tippy-toeing out to quiz probably has some history behind her request; perhaps she felt burned by the lack of funding for a particular idea or concept.

Here's how Jon could respond in a positive way: "Innovation always requires investment. Even the investment of time and mental energy in thinking through the innovation has costs associated with it. Ownership certainly will expect that, when we do make any investment of time or resources, we do so wisely. If we can make the case as a team that our company can take an aggressive step forward with appropriate investment from ownership, I am willing to work with our team to put together a proposal and advance it to Mr. Whitaker."

In looking at Jon's response, think about all the aspects of his likely leadership dashboard that he reinforces with his answer. First, he offered some level of assurance that new ideas were appreciated and embraced. Second, he indicated a willingness to stick his neck out for his team to support their work and innovation. Third, he did, however, reinforce the notion that there would be collective accountability. He was willing to go to management with an idea, but with the understanding that the team would rise and fall to some degree all together. Finally, his reflections regarding the cost of investment and the importance of ongoing levels of innovation speak to his commitment to developing a connected community and real learning power.

Clearly, Jon was being tested as a leader. In this case, his response to the pop quiz helped him demonstrate his commitment to his teammates, share his vision and style choices as a leader, and further clarify to some degree his expectations for those around him. The pop quiz became a valuable learning opportunity for Jon about what his new team feared and for his helpful colleague about what she could expect from Jon in the future.

The pop quiz can take many forms and address a variety of issues. Perhaps a team member will ask for your perspective on outsourcing a particular job function, for instance. An honest, direct answer—even one that creates uneasiness—will create more trust than a reply that is not entirely honest or that sidesteps the issue.

When you get a pop quiz, keep your leadership dashboard in mind. Staying faithful to those beliefs and priorities will help you give consistent pop quiz answers. Your constituents will appreciate your candor, even when they don't like the answers.

Extended Response Exams

In your first 100 days as a leader, you'll be expected to provide extended, thoughtful responses to some of the company's deepest concerns. Some institutions will have more of these concerns; some will have fewer. It's important for you to find a balance between offering extended, thoughtful answers to difficult questions and waiting until you know a bit more about the situation before you commit to an extended answer.

Team members who ask for extended responses hope that you can offer answers and help solve complex problems. They also want to test your competence, hoping that the new leader has the skills to offer thoughtful, detailed responses to complex questions.

Demonstrating your competence is important and can help you build credibility while building deeper levels of understanding and comfort. Even so, it's important that teammates don't see you as the answer person. You might come in with very focused ideas about the company's process and may have creative solutions to problems that have bedeviled the company for years. The most successful companies, however, use leaders to help everyone perform at the highest levels. Requests for extended responses may never stop—a problem that puts you in charge of resolving all the company's major issues. No leader can be a superhero over a long period of time.

Timed Tests

New leaders often find themselves facing difficult, complex questions that need answers early in their tenures. You may not have the luxury of waiting 100 days or more to get to know the institution and make a better-informed decision. These timed tests are among the most stressful aspects of being a new leader. The sudden need to keep or terminate an entire team of professionals or respond to an economic or tactical challenge by totally changing how work is executed can keep new leaders awake at night. Before you take the job, it's helpful to investigate what choices you may need to make right away. Unfortunately, this doesn't always prevent the need to make emergency decisions.

The best way to respond effectively is to keep your leadership dashboard in sight. By following your dashboard, you'll make sure that even quick decisions that have significant impacts are in line with your leadership priorities. Timed tests are arguably more difficult than pop quizzes or extended response exams. The questions are often deep and important to the firm's future, and you don't get much time to answer. If you know who you are as a leader, you're in a much better position to answer successfully.

Demonstration Tests

These are perhaps the most authentic way to assess learning. This test type asks us to show what we know in a real, hands-on manner. You might remember college exams that tested your understanding of scientific processes by asking you to replicate them in a laboratory—tests on which your instructor assessed not only your answers, but also the steps you took to get those results.

New leaders also get demonstration tests. Questioning constituents are interested in your answer, of course, but also in how you approach the question, your response style, and your ability to show your listeners your thinking process. Extra credit goes to leaders who are confident enough to ask constituents what they think about a response and how they might approach the same question. Perhaps the values of asking questions and soliciting other opinions are already on your leadership dashboard.

Don't feel threatened by the testing process. All these tests form an important part of your maturation as a leader in this organization. A lack of tests could signal serious problems with the institution's readiness to learn and evolve. When institutions eagerly test new leaders, it's an indication that constituents want to know and be comfortable with a new manager. As a new leader, you can realistically hope to build the trust and connection necessary to ignite the most significant change. The faster you roll through your pop quizzes, extended response exams, timed tests, and demonstration tests, the faster you can build trust, demonstrate your confidence, and further express your leadership impact goals.

Ten Steps in Building Trust

A thoughtful approach to the testing process helps build trust. Leaders can also take other strategic actions in conjunction with the testing process to reduce fear and create a more comprehensively engaged, focused environment. These suggestions are specifically designed to help a servant leader develop an organization's learning power and create a connected culture.

Use Repetition and Consistency

Your constituents need to become accustomed to seeing you in their environment. They were probably comfortable there before you arrived on the scene. By being mobile, especially early in your first 100 days, you become more familiar. The more often they see you, the more naturally they will accept you. Visibility matters.

Consistency matters, too. Constituents should repeatedly hear you make consistent statements about how you lead, what you believe, and how you intend to support change. That experience helps listeners feel more secure. Even if the message is not an entirely pleasant one—the new leader sets a higher standard than had been set before, for instance, or the new leader plans to take the business in a different direction—teams appreciate hearing clear, consistent information.

Be Transparent

Some leaders arrive with an intention to be completely open and transparent at all times. That's not realistic. Almost every corporate or institutional environment has matters that a leader must keep private. Don't make promises about transparency that you won't be able to keep. Instead, be clear about the parts of your job that allow openness, as well as the ones that don't. Tell questioners that you're not in a position to talk about an issue that needs to stay private. It's an honest answer and will generate less fear than sidestepping the question might.

Ask Questions

Some inexperienced or immature leaders may feel the need to demonstrate competence by behaving as though they know the answers before questions are asked. Constituents typically feel much more comfortable with confident, open leaders who ask honest questions. When you ask questions, you reveal a certain openness; as exchange occurs, you build rapport and trust with those around you.

Follow Through

Your first 100 days will be exhausting and busy. Don't overcommit yourself. There will be moments, however, when a constituent presents a problem that you must follow through on immediately. Carry something that lets you take notes—a pad and pencil, a Blackberry, an iPad, or whatever works for you—on days when you'll frequently move from one place to another, having conversations in hallways and other people's offices.

For example, a casual conversation might alert you to a system that is badly broken and requires immediate attention. You might promise in passing to see what you can do about the problem. Your first 100 days will be overwhelming and confusing, so there's a good chance that you'll forget to follow up if you don't physically note the problem and your promise to do something about it.

Even if you trust your memory, it's wise to begin the habit of writing down new information and disciplining yourself to follow through. Your constituents will soon learn that when you say you will do something, you do it. Even if they don't like your message or don't agree with the action you're taking, there is a certain security in knowing that when you tell them something, they can count on it being true. If they can expect this of you, they may also begin to expect it of themselves and of other team members—thus helping you create accountability throughout the entire organization.

Invest and Commit

It is very difficult to demonstrate deep levels of investment and commitment in the first 100 days. There just isn't enough time. Even in the first 100 days, however, taking every opportunity to demonstrate your commitment, priorities, or investments will help you build trust. Maybe your leadership dashboard includes learning and collaboration as priorities. You demonstrate your commitment to those principles with the decisions you make and the priorities you establish, right from the beginning. If your team sees that you build collaboration time into the workweek, identify key spontaneous learning opportunities, and reframe a critical training expectation during your first 100 days, they'll soon recognize that you are truly committed to investing in these priorities. Again, you're doing what you said you would do, and that builds credibility and establishes trust.

Use Self-Effacing Humor

Be willing to laugh at yourself. It makes you entirely human to everyone around you, building trust and helping you survive the testing process. When you laugh at yourself, you come down a peg and become a little more real. If you're a parent, for example, consider joking about the busy absurdity of raising children. Others in your constituent group will likely relate to your situation and be more likely to identify with you as a result. Identifying with somebody and laughing together is a key technique for releasing stress and building a community. Use humor effectively. Laughing at yourself is more effective than laughing about others, especially at the beginning of your tenure.

Collaborate

Humans are biologically designed to work together.[4] When we collaborate, our brains release endorphins, and we begin to feel good. Actively collaborate with your team. You become a more authentic group member when you build the trust necessary to establish new outcomes.

Engage and Show Emotion

Human beings have complex emotions, and some of us can change emotions on a dime. We can't, however, be immersed in two dramatically different emotional experiences at the same time. It's hard to be profoundly fearful while also feeling wild joy, for instance. One emotion would likely eclipse the other.

We've already talked about the fact that fear impedes learning. One way to create a safe, pro-learning environment is to immerse ourselves in emotions other than fear. Most groups experience emotion as a part of group activities, whether they are explicitly aware of it or not. As a group they may feel bored, engaged, happy, angry, or other emotions, with participants typically sharing the primary emotion.

Any strong, positive emotion can block fear. The ideal emotional state in which to learn and grow, however, is engagement, a balanced state of relaxed alertness. Work to keep your team engaged and focused on the challenge at hand.

Create an Optimal Learning Environment

It's difficult to concentrate on an important task, either individually or in a group, when there is an abundance of noise, it's too hot or too cold, or there is some other distraction. The absence of natural light, low levels of oxygen, enforced sedentary behavior, and even dehydration can keep our brains from operating at optimal efficiency.

A distraction-filled learning environment can create a high level of frustration for those who try to use it. Whenever possible, try to make the working-learning-collaborating environment as comfortable and learner-friendly as possible. Natural light, quiet, comfortable conditions, and the opportunity to move around all help to keep our brains prepared for new material.

Establish Safety Through Nurtured Accountability

At first blush, deadlines and accountability don't sound like much fun. From another angle, however, these structures offer some degree of security by telling us what we must do in order to succeed.

This is especially true when the leader establishes accountability in a nurturing, supportive way. Higher standards combine well with support and resources, often yielding better, more satisfying outcomes. With accountability established and support and additional resources provided, there is also a much greater likelihood that management will pay attention to unsuccessful parts of the development process.

For example, consider the pop quiz discussed earlier, when Jon was asked whether he would support the need for increased levels of funding to support innovation. In his answer, he was careful to let his teammate know that he was willing to support innovation and to stick his neck out for his team. However, he also intimated in his response that together they would own the results. Although his message was subtle, he did make it clear that he wasn't going to simply take a recommendation and charge up the hill. His leadership impact would be driven by the development of a connected culture and the establishment of real learning power, and so the institution has to get comfortable with the freedom and learning power associated with innovation and the real-time reality and necessity that come with accountability measures to keep everyone honest.

A word of warning: in toxic cultures, your attempts to build trust may meet with suspicion and resistance. Don't let failed attempts to build trust persuade you to give up on future attempts. Toxic cultures don't get that way by accident. Your teammates may have experienced many uncomfortable violations of trust in the past, resulting in a suspicious, guarded, disconnected culture. You can build trust in a toxic culture by emphasizing consistency. Your constituents will need to hear your message and see you follow through multiple times before they begin to trust and connect with you. This may take longer than 100 days. Lay your foundation during your first 100 days and continue to reach out, and you'll likely break through in even the toughest environment.

Key Terms

Fear

Testing and trusting

Pop quizzes, extended response exams, timed tests, demonstration tests

Visibility and transparency

Collaboration and engagement

Optimal learning environment

Nurtured accountability

Questions for Reflection

1. Am I ready for all the different types of tests I'm likely to get during my first 100 days?

2. What can I do to build trust with my team?

3. How trusting and connected has this organizational culture been in the past? What might that mean for my leadership strategies?

Chapter 8

The Spiral and CORA Techniques

By THIS POINT IN your life, you've probably realized that you can learn an awful lot by accident. Some of the most memorable learning experiences, in fact, happen entirely by chance, often when the learner isn't necessarily ready for the lesson. Life doesn't always let us study for our most important challenges. The same is true when you lead an organization. Many of your most important learning moments will come quite unexpectedly during your first 100 days, and as the testing and trusting phase continues, you'll need to not only respond to the pop quizzes, extended response exams, demonstration tests, and other challenges issued to you, you'll need ways to test and trust your staff as well.

You can learn strategies that will help you take full advantage of all the learning opportunities that come your way during your first 100 days of leadership. Incorporate these into your leadership style, and you'll be both a better observer and capable of more profound reflection on what your experiences mean for you and those you lead.

As you move through phase 3 of your first 100 days, your ability to quickly and accurately capture the essence of what is going on in your organization will drive, to a great extent, your ability to reflect and then act based on what you observe. Leaders who are ineffective at taking those all-important formative points of analysis often don't spot serious problems in their early stages. They also miss emergent learning opportunities. As you get deeper into your 100 days, and as you prepare to check progress on the 90-day goals set in step 2 of the snapshot process, your ability to accurately gather information will profoundly affect your ability to create a connected culture and build real learning power. This chapter will explore some strategies to help you become a more acute observer of the workings of the systems around you and will describe steps 3 and 4 of the snapshot process: the progress checks.

The 100-Day Timeline

Phase 1: Days 1–6	Phase 2: Days 7–39	Phase 3: Days 40–69	Phase 4: Days 70–100
Creating a Lasting First Impression	Getting in Motion	Testing and Trusting	Celebrating and Looking Forward

Chained to His Desk

Tony was a well-seasoned vice president at a major credit card company. As he was leaving work one day at quarter to six, he found Gerry, one of his newest call center managers, still hard at work, steam rising from a fresh cup of coffee sitting on his desk. Gerry looked exhausted. His eyes were glazed over. The collar on his shirt was undone, his tie loosened. His face was long, with dark circles under his eyes.

"How are you doing?" Tony asked.

"I'm fine, just sticking around trying to keep up," replied Gerry. "I'm having a difficult time keeping up with all my email. I've been stuck behind my desk all day and haven't been able to get out of the call center even once to see how people are doing. My goal for tomorrow is to get all my emails answered, follow up with these reports, and then hopefully begin to make some progress in developing an updated workflow plan to help increase efficiency in the department. There just aren't enough hours in the day."

"You've been stuck behind your desk all day?" Tony asked.

"Yes!" replied Gerry. "I just can't believe the volume of email in this place! I just can't seem to keep up with it. I am trying, however, to get back to everyone in a timely manner."

Gerry is exhausted at the end of the day—even though he hasn't gotten out of his chair. Like many new leaders, Gerry finds his new job overwhelming. He doesn't know where to begin. Everywhere he looks there are new people to know, new challenges to respond to, and an unfamiliar environment to navigate.

One of the reasons leaders like Gerry find themselves overwhelmed is that it's easy to retreat to the familiar in the face of a difficult challenge or uncertainty. In Gerry's case, it's much easier to respond to the crush of emails than it is to walk around and learn in a more organic and authentic manner about the challenges facing his team. Gerry probably isn't avoiding his staff consciously. Even so, answering his daily emails brings him more certainty and a momentary sense of completion—both tough things to find as a new leader with a lot of unanswered questions.

When you're a new leader, your team will try to learn your style and follow your cues. Gerry's reliance on email, therefore, may be sending the message that he prefers to build rapport electronically rather than meet face to face. If that's the message, Gerry's constituents will soon be sending him far more email, because they'll assume that this is his preferred operational mode.

Leaders who sit behind a desk all day can't make a leadership impact. Effective leaders get out and see the work in process. As a new leader, you'll need to be effective in creating influence on the move. That, in turn, will require mastering two major strategies.

Managing by Walking Around

Ken Blanchard has consistently recommended that, whenever possible, leaders need to be mobile, maintaining ongoing and often extemporaneous conversations with constituents from all organizational levels—not just the leader's immediate subordinates.[1] A leader who interacts only with workers at senior job levels, in turn, may send the message that other constituents are less important.

Leaders who walk around can learn about constituents' jobs in an authentic way, rather than relying on workers' descriptions. By asking good questions and learning to watch and listen carefully, leaders can learn a great deal about the work being done. These conversations are also an opportunity for the leader to share ideas and build an ongoing conversation. Mobile leaders also get chances to bring good news and praise workers for doing their jobs well—positive interactions that help build trust and acceptance.

The spiral technique is one good way to manage by walking around.

The Spiral Technique

Many leaders don't manage by walking around very often because they think it's too much work. They fear being pulled into conflicts or conversations that they don't have time to finish. But staying out of conversations can also be damaging. How can leaders reach out more often and more effectively?

The spiral technique can help. To use it, visualize a spiral with three loops, all leading toward a center point. Each loop represents something specific in this leadership model

- **Level-one outside spiral.** At times a broad managerial loop throughout the organization is a helpful trip to take. Stop and have brief conversations before you continue on. If this were all you ever did as a leader, at least you would establish some familiarity within the institution. Others might see you as friendly when you pass by.

- **Level-two loop.** In the second loop of the spiral technique, the leader delves a bit more deeply beyond the organization's outer layer. You might stop and have a brief but substantive conversation—five minutes or less—about a challenge. The second loop takes you closer to the work but does not automatically get you pulled into the deeper conversations you may want to have next.

- **Level-three loop.** At this level, give yourself enough time to have deeper five- to ten-minute conversations. Try to connect at a deep level and truly understand what your constituents think and feel about their jobs. Be an active listener; don't rush.

Leaders can move in and out of the first, second, and third spirals rather quickly, as time and energy dictate. If you have only a short period of time in your day, for example, you can do a quick outside loop and at least connect on a basic level. Between meetings, for example, you may be able to fit in a brief lap around the organization to observe and be present.

If you have a bit more time, you can have a handful of five-minute conversations at level two. This doesn't take much time, especially if you have just a few level-two conversations.

On a perfect day you might have time to make the outside managerial loop, have a few level-two conversations, and end with a couple of level-three conversations, learning more deeply about the people you work with, the jobs they have, and their goals and aspirations. You might be able to share some of your own thoughts and beliefs as well.

A highly organized leader might keep written track of how many first-, second-, and third-loop conversations take place every week or month. Consider making loop observations once a week (or at another specified interval), plus a handful of level-two conversations. Try to have a level-three conversation with each of your constituents perhaps every month or quarter, depending on the number of constituents and the other challenges you have.

This structured approach may feel too formulaic. Keep in mind, though, that it will give you optimal visibility with your team and help you have important conversations with people who matter. Leave your walkabouts to chance, and you'll likely skip important team members and fall out of touch with your workforce. The spiral approach isn't spontaneous, but it can lead to spontaneous outcomes that you wouldn't get through a more casual approach. Think about our example of Gerry at the beginning of the chapter and the degree to which he was chained to his desk. Don't you think he would learn a lot by using the spiraling technique in his call center? Imagine how many spontaneous conversations might emerge if you used this technique.

The CORA Technique

The spiral technique can help you move through the organization in a more deliberate way, taking advantage of even spontaneous holes in your schedule to connect with others. Getting information, however, isn't the same thing as making good use of it. To do that, leaders must hone their abilities to reflect and act on the information they gather.

The CORA technique can help you make better use of your observations. CORA stands for capture, organize, reflect, and act. These actions are ones that leaders in their first 100 days can use to maximize and manage the material they learn by walking around.

- **Capture.** Take notes. No matter how good your memory may be, you'll need a record of the material you learn and observe while you're walking around. Use whatever note-taking method works well for you: a tablet computer, a Dictaphone or other audio recorder, or paper and a pencil. Develop the habit of jotting down notes about what you see, feel, and experience.

  You may think that you are smart enough to simply remember whatever happens, and that may be true (though somewhat unlikely, given the amount of new material leaders encounter in their first 100 days). Even those with good memories learn more from experiences they write about, take notes on, or more actively reflect or record.[2] Your memory of an important interaction will be more substantially engraved in your own gray matter if you develop a habit of taking notes in some form.

  Don't try to take perfect notes. These notes are just for you. Write down everything you can, whether it seems important at the time or not. Casually noted items may mean more later, after reflection.

  As you take notes, be sensitive to your constituents' need for privacy. If they see you furiously recording their words, they may feel you're watching their every move and feel less open with you as a result. Of course, it's also possible that some constituents will see your note-taking as a thoughtful acknowledgment of their comments, particularly if you're jotting a reminder to follow up on a problem someone has mentioned to you. Be sensitive to the situations that might provoke either reaction.

- **Organize.** It's useful to take notes, and even better to organize them. Set up a system that works for you—one that creates an ongoing journal or dialogue with yourself about the things you've heard and observed.

  There are probably as many organizational systems as there are leaders. You might organize the material by subject category, department, geographic area, office, or even job title. I arrange my notes by how they pertain to my dashboard elements. For years I have kept various tabs in notebooks or electronic folders, each one corresponding to my dashboard priorities. I also keep tabs on major projects or initiatives that may be particularly important to the positions I have held. This system lets me attach my notes to pre-existing categories while giving me room to turn notes into new ideas, thoughts, strategies, or potential action items in the leadership areas that matter the most.

If my leadership dashboard includes an emphasis on collaboration and learning, for instance, I might use that as a category for recording feedback on the latest training initiative, which could help me better diagnose and address challenges. My notes help me strategically enrich each aspect of my leadership role, making progress in the areas that matter most.

Sometimes that progress is strategic and deep; sometimes it's simply fixing the organizational equivalent of a leaky faucet. Whether it's a simple to-do or a bigger issue, good notes and organizational systems help leaders follow through on the things that need our attention. Doing that tells constituents that you are interested, engaged, and ready to support them.

- **Reflect.** Take time to think about the things you discover. Using the CORA system in conjunction with the spiral technique gives you lots of conversations and ways to reflect on what you learned in them. Maybe you have level-three conversations with five or six constituents and come away with interesting information, much of it connected to your leadership priorities. Take the time to reflect on the ramifications of what you heard, or those conversations will be of limited value to you. The more comprehensively you reflect and the more thoughtfully you engage, the more likely you are to make use of the information you gather.

  Time spent reflecting will also help you uncover some of your organization's subtext. When you consider what a colleague really meant by a particular comment, you often become a better leader. If you don't take time to reflect, your experiences will come and go without you learning as much as you might from them.

- **Act.** It's all academic until somebody takes action. As you have these important spiral conversations, you'll capture the essence of what's said, organize your thoughts, and reflect on what you heard and how it relates to your leadership mission and company. Not every reflection will inspire action.

  Even so, it's helpful to ask yourself if what you've heard requires action. Did I hear anything today that asks me to rethink my approach? Perhaps the answer is yes—or maybe your reflection offers the seeds of future conversations that will give you additional information and perspective and ultimately drive you to take action.

The spiral technique gets into your constituents' work world, helping you develop a more trusting environment as well as greater degrees of credibility and connection. The CORA technique lets you more strategically organize your thoughts and take more decisive action, based on what you see. Each of these techniques can help you reflect more deeply and take more effective actions during your first 100 days.

Gerry, the call center manager described earlier, might think that somehow he just doesn't have time to execute the level of formal observation. Although this technique may seem laborious and difficult at times, a manager like Gerry can't afford not to invest this time. How will Gerry be able to develop a significant leadership impact if he doesn't become more strategic about going out and actually evaluating the degree to which his work environment is nurturing a connected culture, building real learning power, and working toward the agreed-upon goals? The time Gerry takes to reflect on what he has observed may ultimately make a good portion of the frivolous emails that he is fretting over irrelevant. Innovation may emerge that suddenly washes away a problem that has taken a third of his time every week. Granted, these transcendent innovations don't always happen. However, investing in a more strategic analysis of the environment will pay off for leaders serious about creating a leadership impact that makes a difference.

Performance, Results, and Leadership Impact

The sophisticated data-gathering techniques discussed in this chapter will help you as a leader. They can help others as well. It is perfectly fine to share these techniques with other leaders in your organization. You might even consistently meet as a team to talk about your experiences in applying these strategies.

Ideally, during the reflection process, you will begin to get perspective on your intended leadership impact. If developing a supportive and connected culture is important to you as a leader, for example, you will likely look for it in your regular interactions. With any luck, you'll also know it when you see it.

At this point, you begin to see a return on the investment you made early on by carefully gathering data and getting specific feedback from your constituents about their roles and how they see themselves in their jobs. Your understanding their current perspective on their own and the company's performances puts you in a much better position to observe and reflect on their performance and results.

Revisiting the Snapshot Process

Let's re-examine where we are in the five-step snapshot process and the four phases of your 100 days. Thus far, you've worked to create a good first impression; conducted initial interviews to understand what people do in key positions and the business of your organization (step 1); reflected on the results, made informal observations on existing mental models, and introduced a new mental model if necessary; shared your findings from introductory interviews and informal observations with the team and set in motion 90-day goals to take baby steps toward a new vision (step 2); experienced the inevitable testing and trusting that comes over time; and explored ways to gather information to deepen your understanding of what people do and how they're responding to the changes and your leadership.

By this point, it's important to start checking on those 90-day goals set earlier in the process. Is the team on track? Do adjustments need to be made? What does a current snapshot of the company show?

Step 3: First Progress Check

Step 3 of the snapshot process takes place in phase 3; the second progress check, essentially a repeat of step 3, takes place in phase 4. The progress check is a meeting with the team to revisit the 90-day goals and to examine, together, the team's progress thus far. Both of these meetings can be essentially organized in the same way. However, as you take notes during these meetings, I am sure you will see quite a bit of difference in perception, growth, and progress from phase 3 to phase 4 in the first 100 days. Follow this process for each of these very important snapshot meetings:

1. **Briefly review the results of the step 2 group meeting to share findings and set goals.** This might include an even shorter, highly prioritized, bulleted outline of items addressed in your review and the 90-day goals established through the visioning discussion at the end of the meeting.

2. **Check current perceptions.** It's valuable for the team to revisit some of their discussions and findings from that first meeting. Does the vision still make sense? Was the team too conservative? Too ambitious? Collectively reflecting on these efforts is beneficial and gives leaders an opportunity to think comprehensively about all the conversations they've had with key constituents since arriving.

3. **Ask, Where are we now?** By now, six weeks have passed, and the team still has at least twelve workweeks until the first 100 days are over. Identify what progress has been made to date. In this conversation, constituents should not talk about what they will do. Instead, they should talk with great focus and clarity about what they are currently doing and have done in the last six weeks.

4. **Ask, Where are we going next?** This part of the discussion requires a team to get clear about where it hopes to go in the near future. What can and should happen next to move the team toward its 90-day goals? Identify specific action items that will make a real difference.

The progress check should yield several important outcomes. By re-examining the 90-day goals, the group gets a reminder that there is work to be done and that the organization expects a significant amount of change in a short period of time. The team remembers to own its progress and continues to visualize the steps it can take to shape the vision. In addition to reinforcing the priorities and monitoring the goals established at step 2, the progress check allows team members to illustrate in a concrete way their commitment to the goals and to the change process. It simultaneously tests the commitment and resolve of the leader. Don't totally rethink the initial process and its results. Help the group resist wholesale changes to those initial discussions. Instead, the team should try to reach an increased level of clarity about the vision they are trying to fulfill.

Key Terms

Managing by walking around

The spiral technique

The CORA technique

Capture, organize, reflect, act

Questions for Reflection

1. What are some potential short- and long-term problems that could emerge for a leader who isn't willing to get out and observe and interact with the team and the frontline work they are executing?

2. How does organizing the reflection process in conjunction with observation improve the leader's ability to influence change?

3. How might you actually put the spiral technique to work in the organization in which you work?

4. What tools might you need to apply the CORA technique on a consistent basis? What tools or implements would you use to capture the data you are observing?

5. What have I learned about my leadership impact as a result of the first progress check?

6. In light of the team's current progress toward our 90-day goals, were my expectations too high or too low?

Chapter 9

Maximizing the Growth Zone

IF YOU'RE LIKE A lot of other leaders, you often look back on past jobs and feel that you could have done more. Virtually all of us have had a nagging feeling that more experience, more time, or even a better strategy would have yielded better results. Throughout this book, we have pursued elements that would bring new and improved leadership impacts. With a connected culture and the development of real learning power we can, perhaps, reduce just how often we feel that we have missed the mark.

Maybe a desire to continue improving is part of the reason you're a leader. Not everyone looks back on generally successful performances to imagine how they might have improved. Successful people are always striving for more. At some level, we realize that we've never really taken advantage of our full mental, emotional, and intellectual powers. We know what it feels like to find a new gear, but we don't always know how to find one when we need it. One of the secrets to leading outstanding levels of change and improvement is harnessing more consistently and strategically the real learning power that is associated with a thoughtful leadership impact.

You are now moving into the final phase of your first 100 days. This is the point in your development as a leader when you will be able to take advantage of some of the work you have done thus far, celebrate some successes, and then begin to evaluate what might be some of your most essential priorities moving forward. Up to this point, in developing your leadership impact, you have undoubtedly made great headway in creating a more connected culture by being strategic in your systems of observation, thoughtfully constructing a vision, withstanding testing and trusting, and taking the time to be deeply reflective individually and collectively with your teams. A more connected culture *will* emerge with this level of strategic input and reflection.

Furthermore, you have also, at this point, begun to develop real learning power as your team has worked to clarify your vision, identify your priorities, and place their learning energies more strategically in accordance with your organization's mission and goals.

This chapter, however, takes that process of establishing real learning power to the next level by focusing on your ability to shape a leadership impact by identifying strategic learning growth zones to maximize individual and team potential. Early in this last phase, you'll check progress on the 90-day goals one more time in step 4 of the snapshot process. As you develop new levels of comfort, familiarity, and trust with your team, the process of developing real learning power should take a big, strategic step forward.

A system's ability to learn, adapt, and ultimately succeed is its most important resource. This chapter examines the things leaders can do to maximize growth, improving the performance of everyone involved.

The 100-Day Timeline

Phase 1: Days 1–6	Phase 2: Days 7–39	Phase 3: Days 40–69	Phase 4: Days 70–100
Creating a Lasting First Impression	Getting in Motion	Testing and Trusting	Celebrating and Looking Forward

Harnessing Learning Power for Change

Let's reintroduce Darlene's team:

Jack is 55, originally from Texas, a graduate of Abilene Christian who has spent seventeen years with the company. A grandfather of three, he is affable and highly energetic.

Dave is 41, an African American Muslim from Los Angeles. He has spent seven years with the company. Though willing to work with others, he prefers to work alone. He is quiet, patient, thoughtful, and intelligent.

Kate is 31, was raised and educated in India, and has been in the United States for two years. She is a quiet problem solver with a friendly disposition.

Pam is 32, a proud vegan from Alaska. Confident and energetic, she takes an application-oriented approach to using technology.

Brian is 28, a Harvard-educated Boston native. He has been with the company for eighteen months, is friendly and easy to work with, and has connections with colleagues all over the world.

As Darlene reflected on her first 100 days, she thought about the learning struggles she'd encountered. Dave was often highly stressed and easily distractible, and at times he seemed unable to make significant progress. Jack was never as stressed or frustrated as Dave, but still seemed to get distracted and didn't always focus on essential learning goals. Kate seemed alert and focused on her learning goals, but also highly stressed; Darlene worried that Kate might burn out, in fact. She's seen that highly engaged, highly stressed people sometimes don't last very long. Pam always contributes and doesn't show stress, but Darlene wonders if she could do more. Brian's learning style was similar to Darlene's. Brian was quirky, and at times, his personal affect was humorous at best but still distracting. That said, he had somehow mastered being engaged without letting stress overtake him. This let him relax and make the best decisions in both short- and long-term goals.

Darlene had gotten word earlier in the week that there were some major changes afoot for her department, including changes in their products and some bold alterations to their target market strategy. While Darlene's bosses were clear that these seminal shifts in the business model were non-negotiable, they weren't entirely clear how Darlene and her team were going to continue to execute their work, given these new priorities. Darlene recognized that in order to be responsive to the key changes in work expectations, her team would have to come together and learn a number of new things en route to identifying some innovations and then implementing them. She recognized that this growth effort was dependent on her team's ability to harness their real individual and collective learning potential.

She knew the diversity of her team was a benefit, but she also knew that to fulfill the team's learning potential and move forward in this unique time of change, she had to be thoughtful about her next steps as a leader.

According to learning theory, the optimal learning state for any child or adult occurs when the individual (or team) is relaxed enough to be free of stress and distraction, yet alert enough to be fully engaged in the learning goals at hand.[1] Relaxed alertness is a balancing act, one that makes all the difference in an individual's readiness to learn. You can help your constituents reach relaxed alertness, thereby facilitating their ability to strategically maximize every learning opportunity that comes their way. Moving strategically toward a culture of relaxed alertness supports the definition of leadership impact we have utilized throughout the text. If Darlene is able to facilitate a degree of relaxed alertness on her team, she will construct a more connected culture. Furthermore, by achieving the optimal learning state of relaxed alertness more often, she will harness the individual and collective learning power of her team—which could ultimately result in innovation and increased levels of effectiveness.

Learning and Change

As discussed earlier, to create a leadership impact, you must be thoughtful about your organization's learning conditions and levels of engagement. If the learning atmosphere isn't right, your engagement strategies will likely fail. Furthermore, if individuals are comfortable in their surroundings but aren't focused on the goals at hand, their readiness will be wasted. Your leadership impact depends on your ability to create an environment that is both comfortable and engaging.

Systemic change doesn't occur until learning happens. Nothing really changes until the individuals doing the organization's most important work learn something new and directly apply it to their craft.[2]

Leadership training works when the participants come away with new levels of understanding and apply them to their work. For example, engineers who collaboratively learn something new about an emerging technology are only successful if they then change their behaviors at work, either individually or collectively.

The Ideal Learning State

Neurologists, psychologists, and brain scientists continue to define learning states that stimulate the deepest, most comprehensive levels of learning. Since the early 1990s, they've repeatedly proven that emotion is the secret to learning.[3]

Think about the first time you were in love. Think about all the things you noticed and learned about your beloved. You remember those experiences vividly because you had high levels of emotion about that person, and those emotions stimulated your brain to work at maximum capacity in learning everything it could about your beloved.

If emotion is the key to learning, which emotional states drive us to our most effective learning? It's difficult to answer this question because we all have different learning styles. Some like high levels of engagement and communication when they learn; others need a quiet space; others prefer conversations in a highly interactive environment.

In general, however, the emotional state that keeps us learning at the highest level is relaxed alertness.[4] In a state of relaxed alertness, learners don't feel stress, fear, or the nervous distractions that stop learning in its tracks. But they're not napping; they also experience strong connection and focus.

As a leader in your first 100 days, your best strategy for making a significant leadership impact involves creating an environment that calls forth relaxed alertness. Your team should be relaxed enough to take risks, ask questions, and feel comfortable, while simultaneously being alert and connected, fully engaged in all the nuance and subtext of what they are learning.

Get Relaxed

Stress and fear are typically the emotions that keep teams from being truly relaxed. If you want to stop learning in its tracks, fear is the emotion that will do it![5]

Maybe you see yourself as an exception to this rule. Perhaps you feel that you actually learn more when you are facing a bit of fear and stress. You may find yourself, for example, feeling the pressure of a difficult deadline. You ignite the creative genius within, performing well at the very last minute. Or maybe the fear of failure kept you up all night cramming for college exams and helped you do well in your classes.

In truth, fear itself did not help you learn. Instead, the fear created the opportunities for you to reach heightened engagement levels. Your nervousness or concern, which could have turned into fear, instead became focus, determination, and engagement. You never could have made the deadline or passed the exam if you'd been in a panic for hours or days before the big moment. You may have developed a habit of letting fear *lead you* to engagement, but ultimately it is the engagement that takes you to deep learning.[6]

Fear and stress are bad for you. You know this. Organizations that have high levels of fear and stress typically have employees who are less healthy and less happy than they might otherwise be. Americans in particular are comfortable talking about stress—but stress is really another word for fear. When you find yourself nervously tapping your foot or are crushed for time with pent-up anxiety in your stomach, what you are feeling is fear—in small or large amounts. (Fear is not an all-or-nothing proposition. Small amounts of fear can translate into nervousness or stress.)

You've doubtless seen some of these symptoms of stress in your work environments. Believe it or not, these are also the symptoms of being physically attacked. Fear drives your body into the physiological state of fight-or-flight, readying itself for escape or counterattack.

Symptoms of Stress

- Stiff neck
- Sore back
- Upset stomach
- Racing heart
- Shortness of breath

When you get ready to run or fight for your life, your body goes through survival-oriented changes. It shuts down your digestive system and your immune system; it tightens muscles to prepare for some type of launch; and it races your heart to get blood to your extremities so that you can run, jump, or fight. The blood leaves your brain and goes to your limbs. All of these physiological reactions can happen to small or large degrees, depending on the size of the perceived threat.

If you intend to create a deep, thoughtful leadership impact, you must be cautious about just how often fear emerges in your work environment. If your employees consistently fear you, they are engaging the parts of their brains that shut down learning and creativity.

How can you create relaxation? Building trust goes a long way toward creating a sense of calm. Moreover, your personal demeanor may have to change, particularly if you have a habit of using fear to get people's attention. Because fear is such a powerful tool, some leaders use it to achieve short-term responsiveness and alertness. If you do this, however, the degree to which fear actually slows or prevents learning will become evident in your first 100 days.

Work to move your team into emotional states other than fear and stress. People typically can't feel more than one emotion at a time. Therefore, saturating your team in a positive emotion leaves them with very little capacity to indulge in stress or fear.

This goes beyond just a feel-good approach. For example, when Darlene's team is suddenly faced with an unpredicted and unprecedented challenge, she may elect to pull them together and lay out the challenges ahead. In doing so, she may remind them with a certain degree of engagement and urgency about the successes they have had in the past in pulling together during difficult circumstances. She may individually and collectively reiterate her faith in the team and the presence of pride they have consistently demonstrated when facing a new and unique challenge. She may also encourage them to consider some unique growth opportunities presented by this new hindrance. In all of her discussions, she helps the team experience emotions such as pride and curiosity instead of indulging in stress and fear. When the team is immersed in those positive emotions, the negatives don't have a chance.

Become Alert

There's a big difference between a relaxed work environment and a relaxed cruise ship environment. Some work sessions get silly, perhaps because of fatigue, fun, or distraction. Participants don't really learn the material they've set out to conquer.

Alert engagement is the cure for such nonproductive learning sessions. Unfortunately, alertness is difficult to gauge. We have all attended meetings when we've tried to show a level of focus and engagement that really wasn't there, because we were distracted or not terribly interested in the first place.

We demonstrate alertness in different ways. Some people may sit up and appear highly attentive during a presentation. Others may need to look away from the presenter or down at the table, away from the distractions of the environment or the presenter's face or gestures, to focus on the message. Your team members, too, will demonstrate a wide variety of behaviors that illustrate their relative level of alertness in different ways.[7]

This issue is complicated by the fact that there are multiple levels of engagement. We've all had situations in which we were paying attention, and then suddenly something happened that heightened our awareness levels. People generally spend the least mental effort that a situation requires; reading the newspaper takes fewer mental batteries than learning organic chemistry. Your team members will probably stay only as alert as they need to be.[8]

Want a more alert team? Create a more engaging learning environment, a trick teachers have used for years. They bring their students heightened challenges and more stimulating learning opportunities to increase engagement and learning. Leaders can adopt the same strategy, building and sustaining a stimulating, interesting learning environment to increase alertness and learning—and ultimately create a significant leadership impact.

While creating a more engaging environment isn't easy, there are a handful of simple things that can help. Depending on the type of work you do, your material's complexity, and the number of people involved, consider the following tactics for keeping a team awake and interested, both during a presentation and in general daily work.

- **Introduce novelty.** Novelty stimulates engagement.[9] When a concept is new, we tend to pay more attention to it than if we are deeply associated with it and don't feel we are learning something that matters.

- **Present concepts in broad, simple, contextual terms followed by a more detailed analysis.** This allows the listener to gradually become more acquainted with the concept while making the translation from simple to complex.

- **Offer comparisons.** So much of our learning is based on our ability to look at new learning stimuli and compare it to previous learning, concepts, or mental models.[10] Draw comparisons to elicit the deeper levels of neurological engagement that are required in considering new versus old information.

- **Ask questions.** A person can't simultaneously fall asleep and ask—or answer—a question. The most effective organizations pursue thoughtful answers to carefully presented questions. They might ask questions about service, innovation, or some other metric that defines their work. For example, companies that lose their way may simply ask how they can turn a better profit in the next quarter. A firm that's doing well but looking to do even better might ask, "How can we deliver an entirely unique customer experience than our competition?" or "How can we shock our customers with our levels of follow-up and support?" Those questions are a little surprising, and as such they can stimulate your team to engage in ways they might not on an average day at work.

  A thoughtful leader might also consider asking constituents about their performance and results. As we've said, consistently revisiting performance and results draws more attention to those subjects. Constituents have the chance to revisit habits and ask themselves what actions might improve performance and results, ideally maximizing growth in this area.

  Consider questions to stimulate thinking about what actions affect results. Many well-intended professionals see connections between a particular action and a later result—connections that may be tenuous at best. By asking well-considered questions, you may spark a profitable conversation about real and imagined causality in your organization.

- **Use simulations.** Practice is extremely important in developing new skills or perfecting old ones, with better practice typically leading to better performance. The military uses realistic simulation, for instance, to train soldiers for combat. You might think of some simulations and help your team generate creative solutions in response.

A company I worked with several years ago had one of the world's largest call centers, where they dealt with customer complaints and problems. Over time, their customer agents became less and less consistent in their responses to customer concerns. Changing technology meant that customer agents sometimes responded extemporaneously to customer questions.

To resolve this issue, division managers came up with simulated customer questions for current problems, plus questions they anticipated hearing after making planned changes. By actively debating these questions as a management team, they identified challenges and helped their constituents learn to address them.

- **Issue challenges that raise the bar.** Consider carefully and courageously challenge the status quo. Ask your team "what if" questions about previously unreachable goals. You'll likely get the wheels spinning and create a sense of alertness in those around you. Approach this cautiously, though, because raising the bar can create fear. Ideally, your team should be challenged, highly engaged, and curious. What challenge could you issue that might really stimulate your team? What question could you ask that might ignite deep discussion and engagement?

- **Create structured debate.** Debates with more or less structure are a great way to stimulate alertness and deep thinking. The key is to set up the appropriate structures.

In formal Lincoln-Douglas–style debating, for example, debaters present formal arguments articulating a point-by-point support of their assigned positions. The opposing debaters listen to these presentations, take notes, and reply with carefully articulated, point-by-point responses. Teams that are divided and have reached a stalemate might debate the issue in question. To really stimulate alertness, ask the teams to switch their arguments and present the case that's in direct conflict with their previously stated opinions. This strategy can sometimes help opponents better understand the people who disagree with them. In the long run, it can also help them articulate their own positions.

The debate process, which involves going back and forth in an organized, respectful, perhaps timed fashion, creates virtually unmatched levels of engagement in the participants. Debates take time, of course, and time is at a premium in every organization. The learning that takes place during a debate, however, is nearly always worth the investment.

- **Shake it up.** Ken Blanchard tells a revealing story about a training session he led. On the last day of training, the team expected a rigorous day of learning. Instead, the company president rolled in an army of caterers and hosted an unexpected party. The president told everyone how much he appreciated their efforts. The company never forgot that moment of frivolity, forevermore known there as *Ferris Bueller's Day Off*.

  Knocking off work is one way of shaking things up, though of course you can't use this tactic too often if you want to remain competitive. Think of some other activities your team won't expect. If you have a routine built into your sessions, try asking them to do new things during that time.

Learning is a delicate balance of discipline and focus, keeping the learners a bit off balance but also engaged. There's no perfect way to do it, but there are many strategies that can enhance your team's learning experience.

Thinking Strategically About Relaxed Alertness

Let's revisit Darlene's team and their various abilities to be relaxed and alert. Since ultimately her goal is to create a leadership impact that is driven by relaxed alertness, we know she has some work to do with some of the members of her team. As we profile each of her team members, see if you can recognize some of these characteristics of people in your own organization.

- **Dave.** Not relaxed, not alert. As you have learned, relaxed alertness is the key to learning. Unfortunately, Dave is neither consistently relaxed nor alert. He is always on edge, and his emotions never take him toward that deep level of engagement that allows learning and the ability to make a more significant contribution.

- **Jack.** Relaxed, but not alert. Jack appears comfortable in his skin and is a fun person to be around. However, Jack is not consistently alert and engaged. The fact that Jack is not distracted by stress and fear is great. However, that's of little value to Darlene and the company if Jack does not learn to take that sense of relaxation and then empower it with a more alert focus.

- **Kate.** Not relaxed, but alert. Many of you reading this book may fall into this category. High achievers are often extremely alert and focused, but not very relaxed. Kate can probably add value to the company thanks to hard work, focus, and, at times, innovative ideas. However, Kate's emotional tenor of being on edge and stressed influences how others feel—and others may not be as capable as Kate (or you) in handling that stress and remaining alert. Therefore, even if Kate is making a contribution, Darlene has to be worried about Kate's long-term viability and her impact on others in creating a more toxic environment.

- **Pam.** Relaxed and alert, to a degree. Pam is solid, but she isn't an innovator. She needs the company of peers to really engage. Darlene needs to find ways to challenge Pam.

- **Brian.** Relaxed and alert, like Darlene. He doesn't find himself unusually stressed out during moments of trial or tension and is able to switch on his engagement and be challenged and focused in resolving the issues at hand. This is the ideal learning state.

While Darlene can't always create the perfect learning conditions, she can set up team learning or collaboration time to provide engaging learning opportunities in a rigorous (yet safe) environment. She could, for example, challenge her team to come up with a new and much-needed innovation to resolve a problem or maximize an opportunity. Giving the team members time to thoughtfully brainstorm—so they know they will be able to revisit their ideas or positions—would help create the state of relaxed alertness that allows engagement to turn into deep learning and innovation.

Step 4: Second Progress Check

We're now ready for step 4 of the snapshot process. Again, the progress check is a meeting with the team to revisit the 90-day goals and to examine, together, the team's progress thus far—to take a snapshot of the current situation. By now, the team has just a few workweeks until the first 100 days are over. Identify what progress has been made to date, and what is left to accomplish. Follow the same process:

1. Briefly review the results of the step 2 group meeting to share findings and set goals, as well as the results of the step 3 progress check.

2. Check current perceptions.

3. Ask, "Where are we now?"

4. Ask, "Where are we going next?"

Three Enduring Questions to Maximize Growth

One of the mistakes leaders often make when attempting to support deeper team learning is neglecting to identify what the team already knows and its readiness to move forward to the next learning objective. While you may hope that your team is ready for a deeper learning challenge by this stage in the snapshot process, you can be more strategic in these efforts by asking the following three formative questions:

1. **What do we know?** When we ask this foundational question, we are not just talking about competitive knowledge. We are also talking about individual and shared skill sets. Darlene's team might want to ask, "What do we know as a team about what we're doing, and what are the likely future effects of that?" Understanding where we are helps us create the future we want.

2. **What are we ready to learn?** There's no sense in presenting unrealistic challenges or asking for things that are truly beyond the team's capacity. By doing that, Darlene would invite frustration. Realistic learning goals, however, are essential to future growth. For example, Darlene's team may recognize that they lack technological skills or information about customers, marketing,

future growth opportunities, international markets, or emerging trends. They can then move to fill those gaps. Knowing what you know is important. Identifying what you don't know is also key.

3. **Where is our growth zone?** Learners progress most effectively when they have a challenge that is rigorous and engaging but not so difficult that they can't see progress. What goals are doable for your team, yet represent a bit of a stretch?

Key Terms

Fear

Growth learning zone

Learning conditions

Levels of engagement

Relaxed alertness

Stress

Simulations

Structured debate

Questions for Reflection

1. Overall, how aware is my team of their individual and group learning capacities?

2. Was it difficult for my team to identify which learning objectives would be most germane to their organizational roles? If yes, what does that tell me about my work as a leader?

3. What am I ready to learn as a leader? How can my growth change me and those I serve?

4. What have I learned about my leadership impact as a result of the second progress check?

5. In light of the team's current progress toward our 90-day goals, were my expectations too high or too low?

Chapter 10

Achieving
Gradual Clarity

AT THE BEGINNING OF this book, we talked about Michelangelo's habit of looking at a large uncut marble block and envisioning the beautiful piece of art within. Leaders today give their teams chisels and collectively create an artistic vision.

In the past, of course, leaders called all the shots. It's still not easy for many leaders to let constituents have a substantial hand in shaping goals and strategies. In allowing others to be actively involved in constructing and pursuing a vision, today's leaders live with greater degrees of ambiguity. It's their job to clarify the group's goals, asking the team to consistently revisit its collective vision.

By this point in your first 100 days, the fog has lifted. You can look back at earlier phases and reflect on just how much you know now about your organization, its strengths and weaknesses, the emerging capacities of your team, and some of the possibilities that lie ahead. This is an exciting time in that you can see the impact you have made, thanks to the strategic steps you have taken in your first 100 days.

The good news is that you are not the only one achieving this clarity. Indeed, your colleagues have likewise gotten clear during this induction process, and by and large, they too have greater clarity about their roles in the organization and the priorities and possibilities that lie ahead. The emergence of a more connective culture and the development of real learning power will gain momentum with this new clarity.

In this chapter, we will address some steps you can take to further your leadership impact by taking direct action to bring clarity to the vision and direction established thoroughly in phase 2. We'll also take the fifth and final step in our snapshot process, the 100-day culmination.

The 100-Day Timeline

Phase 1: Days 1–6	Phase 2: Days 7–39	Phase 3: Days 40–69	Phase 4: Days 70–100
Creating a Lasting First Impression	Getting in Motion	Testing and Trusting	Celebrating and Looking Forward

Kiara's Journal

Kiara is a new product development manager finishing her first 100 days at a large for-profit online learning institution. Like so many other workers in this company, her youth wasn't as much of a hindrance as it might be in other situations; her digital-native ability to utilize technology makes her a valuable asset in this market.

In addition to finishing her first 100 days in the job, Kiara is also finishing a master's program in public administration. The academic stimulation in combination with the frontline leadership experience has proven helpful for her. Throughout her leadership journey, Kiara has kept a journal on her laptop. She didn't share this journal with anybody; she simply used it as an opportunity to reflect on her thoughts and ideas throughout her first 100 days. Looking back now, she is able to see just how much she and her team of product developers have grown during their time working together.

Toward the end of phase 1, Kiara identified some key priorities associated with her job and created her leadership dashboard. Now she marvels at how much more precise she has become less than 100 days later. But she can also see that early in her first 100 days, she had already begun forming an understanding of the company's current position and a vision for what was possible in the days ahead.

Patience has not always been Kiara's strong suit. Looking back at her journal entries, she sees entries typed in virtually all capital letters, peppered with exclamation points. In those moments she was frustrated by her lack of clarity about her job and exactly what needed to be done. Now that the first 100 days are over, however, she finds herself more at peace with the fact that much of what she had to do as a leader revealed itself gradually. It just took some time for the picture to get clearer in her mind and, perhaps, in the minds of those she worked with throughout this leadership change.

As Kiara reflects on day 101 and beyond, she recognizes that her journey in leadership will only bring greater levels of clarity if she continues to be thoughtful and strategic. Even the act of keeping the journal, it seems to her now, has illuminated her path forward.

Making a strong leadership impact is fueled to a great extent by the clarity everyone in the organization has about the institution's goals, objectives, and pathway forward. That said, absolute clarity may be an unattainable standard, and new leaders must learn to be patient. There are undoubtedly going to be some blind spots and some moments of confusion in the early phases of the first 100 days. Becoming comfortable with the idea that clarity only emerges gradually will help leaders be more effective at making a lasting leadership impact.

Four Keys to Clarity

Leaders need four essential concepts to be comfortable with initial ambiguity and growing understanding.

Accept Starting With That Large Uncut Block of Marble

It's tempting to look for absolute clarity on the first day of your leadership position. But developing clarity takes time. To be successful in the first 100 days, you must be comfortable with ambiguity around that large marble block that is your unfinished leadership impact. Some leaders have very specific ideas about what they hope to create, or they might inherit a half-finished sculpture. Other leaders may be starting from ground zero, with virtually no clarity about institutional direction. Ultimately, patience becomes paramount. Some organizations truly are a huge block of unfinished marble, and that's the leader's starting point. It's important to acknowledge this without becoming frustrated.

Accept a Partially Completed Work of Art

Many of us seek completion. (It's a common trait in Western culture.) Try to relax and live with uncertainty. You may have a lot of work to do in getting your team to chisel and sculpt together as one. They may not have a lot of collective clarity about what they are trying to create. No matter where they start, though, they'll begin to shape a vision during the first 100 days. It will emerge gradually, incompletely at first. It's not easy for task- and outcome-oriented leaders to live with a fuzzy, uncertain state of incompleteness. Remember that being patient will pay dividends. In many cases, rushing the team or organization toward a false sense of clarity will not enhance the emerging leading and learning process.

A partially completed work of art doesn't signal that its creators decided nothing at all about the end product—only that the final decisions are yet to come. To begin, a leader and team can often decide on some non-negotiable goals. The team may be clear about the service they hope to deliver, for instance, or about at least some of their values and beliefs. Additional steps toward clarity will help focus these substantial first steps.

Let Other People Make an Impact, Too

Leaders may talk a great game about inclusion and participation. Too often, however, when push comes to shove, they're reluctant to let other people share the lead.

Some leaders, for example, will try to facilitate a collaborative environment. As their team begins to reformulate its vision for what's possible, the leader steps in and takes center stage on the important shaping process. The degree to which you allow others to shape the vision is driven to some extent by the work's complexity and by your team's competence and abilities. That said, the best leaders promote leadership and learning as qualities that the entire organization can access.

This requires trust and a light hand on the wheel. Leaders have a great deal of confidence in themselves; they may also feel that their reputations are on the line as they work with teams they're still getting to know. That makes it hard to relinquish control. Try to trust that new innovations can emerge, especially if you nurture them appropriately. You'll build greater levels of creativity, ownership, and accountability when you let other people lead, and you'll ultimately reach better outcomes.

Live With Mistakes

You and your team can't be creative if you're not allowed to make mistakes. Learning is at least partially a trial-and-error process, and learners in your organization need to manage their own learning and make some mistakes along the way. Trusting your team to do this is a big step for a leader, particularly when other supervisors, boards of directors, and other authority figures are watching your progress. Allowing and reflecting on mistakes helps people increase their abilities to learn and grow. In ideal situations, leaders let constituents make mistakes, but not the most disastrous possible mistakes. It's not easy to find this balance, but it's well worth the effort.

Step 5: 100-Day Culmination

On or about day 100, host a celebration, and reflect on how the team has done during your first 100 days. Revisit the questions, Where are we now, and where are we going? Identify the good work that has come out of the collaborative process, and recognize the outstanding contributions your constituents have made. A celebration also reinforces the new direction and confirms that change is really under way.

You should give credit to everyone but yourself, of course. Even so, your entire organization will see that you have led the group to greater degrees of clarity about its destination and have helped create a team that is much more self-aware and reflective.

Don't make this culminating celebration revolve around the fact that you have been on the job 100 days. Instead, guide the conversation around the idea that 100 days have passed since *the team came together* and refocused its energy. This shouldn't be a celebration of your leadership efforts to save the day, but instead a celebration of 100 days of working together to seek something new. It's an important distinction that keeps the focus on the team, not the leader.

Evaluating the Snapshot Process

Ideally, you'll see improvement and evolution at each step of the snapshot process, in each discussion. This is a developmental process, and you may find that although your first 100 days have come and gone, you still have a long road ahead in building your team's capacity to work together and understand where they are and where they are going.

This snapshot process is just your starting point. An organization that was struggling before you got there won't resolve its problems just because you've arrived. In fact, you'll spend many of your first 100 days just uncovering company issues—time well spent, as you can't move past obstacles without first discovering them. Far too many leaders stay relatively oblivious to challenges, and ultimately problems go unaddressed. You'll continue taking snapshots, in one way or another, long after your first 100 days.

To help judge the success of your first five snapshots, consider these five questions.

1. Was everyone involved in shaping the vision?

2. Is the team able to convey a clear vision? Did it get clearer with each subsequent discussion?

3. Is the team successfully identifying the problems keeping the organization from making progress?

4. Is the leading and learning culture improving? Are people working better together as a group?

5. Is the team improving its individual and collective leadership and capacity for change?

Look for clarity about your leadership impact as you consider how your organization is evolving. Is its learning power growing? Is it developing a more connected culture? What challenges have appeared? Each snapshot should move you further down the road toward addressing problems and refining your leadership impact.

As a leader, you should come away from snapshot discussions with a clear sense of performance and results. Does each snapshot conversation lead us to better ideas about our performance levels? Are we clear about how we achieved them? Have we gotten away from the assumption that certain actions will automatically create certain outcomes?

The strategies in this book will accelerate a leader's progress. Even so, clarity, connection, and momentum all take time to build. A leader needs a careful sense of balance, employing patience as well as a willingness to push the envelope. Over time, more clarity and skill will develop—in both leader and team.

Key Terms

The leader as artist

Clarity

Questions for Reflection

1. How can having patience with gradual levels of clarity help me get to my destination more quickly?

2. How does the analogy of the artist's chisel in reference to the leader's role differ from the traditional concept of what it means to lead?

3. Why is an artist's perspective more effective for organizations today?

The 100-Day Timeline

Phase 1: Days 1–6	Phase 2: Days 7–39	Phase 3: Days 40–69	Phase 4: Days 70–100
Creating a Lasting First Impression	Getting in Motion	Testing and Trusting	Celebrating and Looking Forward

ON DAY 101 YOU might find yourself exhilarated, exhausted, informed, and ready for more! You will likely have many unanswered questions. Let them inspire you to learn more about the organization you serve and about your own journey as a leader. As you have no doubt discovered, being a leader offers you a wonderfully interesting, demanding, and emotionally engaging learning opportunity.

Your first 100 days may have given you a view of your organization's strengths—and its problems. This is just the beginning. You've established a foundation from which to build and refine your leadership influence. By keeping your dashboard in mind, you'll more often than not take actions that reflect your most important purposes.

During your first 100 days you've also captured the essence of a new vision and learned what it means to construct that vision. Your capacity to know your history, comprehend mental models, and acknowledge the current context are the three most important components of your company's vision. The more strategically you keep these factors in mind, the better you'll understand today's visions and shape those of tomorrow.

You'll be tested at numerous points on your journey through your first 100 days—and beyond. Look at this testing process as a natural evolutionary component of developing a connected culture and enhanced learning power, and be patient with both the process and with those who test you. These moments of testing enhance the clarity needed to enrich your vision. By applying these techniques and striving for maximum learning and growth, you'll find that day 101 brings a great deal of clarity about where you've been, how you got there, and what's left to do.

Thanks to all these growth opportunities at every phase, by now, you will have made an undeniable leadership impact on the organization. On one level, the impact will be felt by everyone in the institution as they begin to appreciate being part of a more connected culture that allows leadership to emerge from all corners of the organization. By this point, this connected culture should have started to create a more trusting and supportive environment that, ultimately, responds better when challenged. While some of these challenges will come from outside the organization in the form of unique hindrances and opportunities, thanks to a more thoughtfully constructed, connected culture, your teams will be better able to negotiate internal levels of disagreement and recognize that these conflicts all represent potential growth opportunities.

On another level, your leadership impact will be felt in the explosion of real learning power throughout the organization. With greater clarity, better communication, and more systematic opportunities to gather information and collaborate, learning gains considerable momentum. Furthermore, by being strategic in identifying growth opportunities and getting clearer about the new learning that is necessary to improve, you will have established real learning power that will allow your organization to take on challenges that might have seemed insurmountable in the past.

I hope your first 100 days have been enriching and enjoyable for you. You have undoubtedly shared a lot with those around you, and hopefully everyone you have touched has become better at what they do, thanks to your emergence in this new role. Furthermore, I hope that you, too, as a more open and deeply reflective leader, have benefited from the processes described in this book and from the opportunities you have had to work with those around you in this growth journey.

You've reached day 101. Go forward with courage.

Notes

Introduction: Everyone, Grab a Chisel!

1. Alexei V. Egorov, Klaus Unsicker, and Oliver von Bohlen und Halbach, "Muscarinic Control of Graded Persistent Activity in Lateral Amygdala Neurons," *European Journal of Neuroscience* 24, no. 11 (2006): 3183–3194.

Chapter 1: Creating a Leadership Impact

1. Robert K. Greenleaf, *Servant Leadership: A Journey Into the Nature of Legitimate Power and Greatness* (New York: Paulist Press, 1977).

2. Ken Blanchard, *The One Minute Manager* (New York: Berkley Books, 1983).

3. Matthew Garner, Karin Mogg, and Brendan P. Bradley, "Orienting and Maintenance of Gaze to Facial Expressions in Social Anxiety," *Journal of Abnormal Psychology* 115, no. 4 (2006): 760–770.

4. Gayle H. Gregory and Terrence Parry, *Designing Brain-Compatible Learning*, 3rd ed. (Thousand Oaks, CA: Corwin Press, 2006).

Chapter 2: Designing Your Leadership Dashboard

Chapter 3: Creating a Lasting First Impression

Chapter 4: Taking a Company Snapshot

Chapter 5: Matching Mental Models

1. Casey Reason, *Leading a Learning Organization: The Science of Working With Others* (Bloomington, IN: Solution Tree Press, 2010).

2. John W. Creswell, *Research Design: Qualitative, Quantitative, and Mixed Methods Approaches* (Thousand Oaks, CA: SAGE, 2009).

3. Reason, *Leading a Learning Organization.*

4. Robert W. Levenson, "Autonomic Specificity and Emotion," in Richard J. Davidson, Klaus R. Scherer, and H. Hill Goldsmith (eds.), *Handbook of Affective Sciences* (New York: Oxford University Press, 2003), 212–224.

Chapter 6: Building a Better Vision

1. Mary E. Braine, "The Role of the Hypothalamus, Part 1: The Regulation of Temperature and Hunger," *British Journal of Neuroscience Nursing* 5, no. 2 (2009): 66–72. Jarrod Moss, Kenneth Kotovsky, and Jonathan Cagan, "The Role of Functionality in the Mental Representations of Engineering Students: Some Differences in the Early Stages of Expertise," *Cognitive Science* 30 (2006): 65–93.

2. Curtis J. Bonk, *The World Is Open: How Web Technology Is Revolutionizing Education* (San Francisco: Jossey-Bass, 2009).

Chapter 7: Testing and Trusting

1. Bruce H. Lipton, *The Biology of Belief: Unleashing the Power of Consciousness, Matter and Miracles* (Carlsbad, CA: Hay House, 2008).

2. Randy J. Larsen, "Toward a Science of Mood Regulation," *Psychological Inquiry* 11, no. 3 (2000): 129–141. Dianne M. Tice and Ellen Bratslavsky, "Giving in to Feel Good: The Place of Emotion Regulation in the Context of General Self-Control," *Psychological Inquiry* 11, no. 3 (2000): 149–159.

3. Gwendolyn E. Wood et al., "Chronic Immobilization Stress Alters Aspects of Emotionality and Associative Learning in the

Rat," *Behavioral Neuroscience* 122, no. 2 (2008): 282–292. Rose Sprinkle et al., "Fear in the Classroom: An Examination of the Teachers' Use of Fear Appeals and Students' Learning Outcomes," *Communication Education* 55, no. 4 (2006): 389–402. Lipton, *The Biology of Belief.*

4. Carla Hannaford, *Playing in the Unified Field: Raising and Becoming Conscious, Creative Human Beings* (Salt Lake City: Great River Books, 2010).

Chapter 8: The Spiral and CORA Techniques

1. Ken Blanchard, *Leading at a Higher Level: Blanchard on Leadership and Creating High-Performing Organizations* (Upper Saddle River, NJ: FT Press, 2009).

2. Mary Ann Foley, et al., "Remembering More Than Meets the Eye: A Study of Memory Confusions About Incomplete Visual Information," *Memory* 15, no. 6 (2007): 616–633. Elizabeth Marsh, "Retelling Is Not the Same as Recalling: Implications for Memory," *Current Directions in Psychological Science* 16, no. 1 (2007): 16–20.

Chapter 9: Maximizing the Growth Zone

1. Renata Nummela Caine et al., *12 Brain/Mind Learning Principles in Action: The Fieldbook for Making Connections, Teaching, and the Human Brain* (Thousand Oaks, CA: Corwin Press, 2005).

2. Reason, *Leading a Learning Organization.*

3. Gregory and Parry, *Designing Brain-Compatible Learning.*

4. Caine et al., *12 Brain/Mind Learning Principles.*

5. Wood et al., "Chronic Immobilization Stress." Sprinkle et al., "Fear in the Classroom" Lipton, *The Biology of Belief.*

6. Reason, *Leading a Learning Organization.*

7. Ibid.

8. Caine et al., *12 Brain/Mind Learning Principles.*

9. Reason, *Leading a Learning Organization.*

10. Ibid.

Chapter 10: Achieving Gradual Clarity

Epilogue: Day 101

Bibliography

Blanchard, Ken. *The One Minute Manager.* New York: Berkley Books, 1983.

Blanchard, Ken. *Leading at a Higher Level: Blanchard on Leadership and Creating High-Performing Organizations.* Upper Saddle River, NJ: FT Press, 2009.

Bonk, Curtis J. *The World Is Open: How Web Technology Is Revolutionizing Education.* San Francisco: Jossey-Bass, 2009.

Braine, Mary E. "The Role of the Hypothalamus, Part 1: The Regulation of Temperature and Hunger." *British Journal of Neuroscience Nursing* 5, no. 2 (2009): 66–72.

Burns, Dan. *The First 60 Seconds: Win the Job Interview Before It Begins.* Naperville, IL: Sourcebooks, 2009.

Caine, Renata Nummela, Geoffrey Caine, Carol Lynn McClintic, and Karl J. Klimek. *12 Brain/Mind Learning Principles in Action: The Fieldbook for Making Connections, Teaching, and the Human Brain.* Thousand Oaks, CA: Corwin Press, 2005.

Creswell, Jown W. *Research Design: Qualitative, Quantitative, and Mixed Methods Approaches.* Thousand Oaks, CA: SAGE, 2009.

Deming, W. Edwards. *Out of the Crisis.* Cambridge, MA: MIT Press, 2000.

Egorov, Alexei V., Klaus Unsicker, and Oliver von Bohlen und Halbach. "Muscarinic Control of Graded Persistent Activity in Lateral Amygdala Neurons." *European Journal of Neuroscience* 24, no. 11 (2006): 3183–3194.

Foley, Mary Ann, Hugh J. Foley, Rachel Scheye, and Angelica M. Bonacci. "Remembering More Than Meets the Eye: A Study of Memory Confusions About Incomplete Visual Information." *Memory* 15, no. 6 (2007): 616–633.

Friedman, Thomas L. *The World Is Flat: A Brief History of the Twenty-First Century.* New York: Farrar, Straus and Giroux, 2005.

Garner, Matthew, Karin Mogg, and Brendan P. Bradley. "Orienting and Maintenance of Gaze to Facial Expressions in Social Anxiety." *Journal of Abnormal Psychology* 115, no. 4 (2006): 760–770.

Greenleaf, Robert K. *Servant Leadership: A Journey Into the Nature of Legitimate Power and Greatness.* New York: Paulist Press, 1977.

Gregory, Gayle H., and Terrence Parry. *Designing Brain-Compatible Learning,* 3rd ed. Thousand Oaks, CA: Corwin Press, 2006.

Hannaford, Carla. *Playing in the Unified Field: Raising and Becoming Conscious, Creative Human Beings.* Salt Lake City: Great River Books, 2010.

Johnson, Spencer, and Ken Blanchard. *Who Moved My Cheese? An Amazing Way to Deal With Change in Your Work and in Your Life.* New York: Putnam, 1998.

Larsen, Randy J. "Toward a Science of Mood Regulation." *Psychological Inquiry* 11, no. 3 (2000): 129–141.

Levenson, Robert W. "Autonomic Specificity and Emotion." In Richard J. Davidson, Klaus R. Scherer, and H. Hill Goldsmith (eds.), *Handbook of Affective Sciences* (pp. 212–224). New York: Oxford University Press, 2003.

Lipton, Bruce H. *The Biology of Belief: Unleashing the Power of Consciousness, Matter and Miracles.* Carlsbad, CA: Hay House, 2008.

Marsh, Elizabeth J. "Retelling Is Not the Same as Recalling: Implications for Memory." *Current Directions in Psychological Science* 16, no. 1 (2007): 16–20.

Michelangelo. (n.d.). Great-Quotes.com. Accessed December 14, 2001. http://www.great-quotes.com/quote/43205.

Moss, Jarrod, Kenneth Kotovsky, and Jonathan Cagan. "The Role of Functionality in the Mental Representations of Engineering Students: Some Differences in the Early Stages of Expertise." *Cognitive Science* 30 (2006): 65–93.

Reason, Casey. *Leading a Learning Organization: The Science of Working With Others.* Bloomington, IN: Solution Tree Press, 2010.

Senge, Peter M., Nelda H. Cambron-McCabe, Timothy Lucas, Bryan Smith, Janis Dutton, and Art Kleiner. *Schools That Learn: A Fifth Discipline Fieldbook for Educators, Parents, and Everyone Who Cares About Education.* New York: Doubleday, 2000.

Sprinkle, Rose, Stephen Hunt, Cheri Simonds, and Mark Comadena. "Fear in the Classroom: An Examination of the Teachers' Use of Fear Appeals and Students' Learning Outcomes." *Communication Education* 55, no. 4 (2006): 389–402.

Tice, Dianne M., and Ellen Bratslavsky. "Giving in to Feel Good: The Place of Emotion Regulation in the Context of General Self-Control." *Psychological Inquiry* 11, no. 3 (2000): 149–159.

Vaynerchuk, Gary. *The Thank You Economy.* New York: Collins Business, 2011.

Wolfe, Patricia. *Brain Matters: Translating Research Into Classroom Practice.* Alexandria, VA: Association for Supervision and Curriculum Development, 2001.

Wood, Gwendolyn E., Erin H. Norris, Elizabeth Waters, Jeremiah T. Stoldt, and Bruce S. McEwen. "Chronic Immobilization Stress Alters Aspects of Emotionality and Associative Learning in the Rat." *Behavioral Neuroscience* 122, no. 2 (2008): 282–292.

Index

About the Author

CASEY REASON has worked with leaders from all over the world on breakthrough strategies designed to improve performance and overcome resistance to change. His easily applied approaches are founded on the emerging body of research in brain science and adult learning theory. Reason has worked with clients throughout the United States, Switzerland, and New Zealand, and is president of Highpoint Learning, an Arizona-based consulting company.